IN THE NAME OF
ALLAH
THE ALL-COMPASSIONATE, ALL-MERCIFUL

The Purpose of Creation

- Title: The Purpose of Creation
- Author: Dr. Abu Ameenah Bilal Philips
- New Revised Edition 2 (2006)
- Layout: IIPH, Riyadh, Saudi Arabia
- Filming & Cover Designing: Samo Press Group

The Purpose of Creation

الغاية من الخلق

Dr. Abu Ameenah Bilal Philips

INTERNATIONAL ISLAMIC PUBLISHING HOUSE

King Fahd National Library Cataloging-in-Publication Data

Philips, Abu Ameenah Bilal
The purpose of creation. / Abu Ameenah Bilal Philips .- Riyadh, 2006

...p ; 22 cm

ISBN : **9960-850-83-8**

1- Faith (Islam) 2- Islamic theology I-Title

240 dc 1424/6811

ISBN: **9960-850-83-8**
Legal deposit no. 1424/6811

International Islamic Publishing House (IIPH)
P.O.Box 55195 Riyadh 11534, Saudi Arabia
Tel: 966 1 4650818 - 4647213 - Fax: 4633489
E-Mail: iiph@iiph.com.sa - www.iiph.com.sa

TABLE OF CONTENTS

TRANSLITERATION CHART

أ	a
آ . ى	â
ب	b
ت	t
ة	h or t (when followed by another Arabic word)
ث	th
ج	j
ح	ḥ
خ	kh
د	d
ذ	dh
ر	r
ز	z
س	s
ش	sh
ص	ṣ
ض	ḍ
ط	ṭ

ظ	dh
ع	‘
غ	gh
ف	f
ق	q
ك	k
ل	l
م	m
ن	n
هـ – ه – ـه	h
و	w
و (as vowel)	oo
ي	y
ي (as vowel)	ee
ء	’ (Omitted in initial position)

َ	Fatḥah	a
ِ	Kasrah	i
ُ	Ḍammah	u
ّ	Shaddah	Double letter
ْ	Sukoon	Absence of vowel

INTRODUCTION

The purpose of creation is a topic that puzzles every human being at some point in his or her lifetime. Everybody, at some time or another, asks themselves the question "Why do I exist?" or "For what purpose am I here on earth?"

The variety and complexity of the intricate systems which constitute the fabric of both human beings and the world in which they exist indicate that there must have been a Supreme Being who created them. Design indicates a designer. When human beings come across footprints on a beach, they immediately conclude that a human being had walked by there some time previously. No one imagines that the waves from the sea settled in the sand and by chance produced a depression looking exactly like human footprints. Nor do humans instinctively conclude that they were brought into existence without a purpose. Since purposeful action is a natural product of human intelligence, humans conclude that the Supreme Intelligent Being who created them must have done so for a specific purpose. Therefore, human beings need to know the purpose of their existence in order to make sense of this life and to do what is ultimately beneficial for them.

Throughout the ages, however, there has been a minority among humans who have denied the existence of God. Matter, in their opinion, is eternal and mankind is merely a chance product of accidental combinations of its elements. Consequently, to them, the question "Why did God create man?" had and still has no answer. According to them, there simply is no purpose to existence. However, the vast majority of humankind over the ages have believed and continue to believe in the existence of a Supreme Being who created this world with a purpose. For them it was, and still is, important to know about the Creator and the purpose for which He created human beings.

The Answer

To answer the question "Why did God create man?" it must first be determined from which perspective the question is being asked. From the point of view of God it would mean, "What caused God to create human beings?" While from the human point of view it would mean "For what purpose did God create humans?" Both points of view represent aspects of the intriguing question "Why do I exist?" In the following pages, both aspects of the question will be explored based on the clear picture painted by divine revelation. This is not a topic for human speculation, because human guesswork cannot possibly produce the whole truth in this matter. How can human beings intellectually deduce the reality of their existence when they can hardly understand how their own brain or its higher entity, the mind, functions? Consequently, the many philosophers who have speculated on this question down through the ages have come up with innumerable answers, all of which are based on assumptions which cannot be proven. Questions on this topic have even led a number of philosophers to claim that we do not really exist and that the whole world is imaginary. For example, the Greek philosopher Plato (428-348 BC) argued that the everyday world of changeable things, which man comes to know by the use of his senses, is not the primary reality, but is a shadow world of appearances.[1] Many others, as was previously mentioned, claimed and continue to claim that there is no purpose for the creation of humans at all. According to them, Human existence is merely a product of chance. There can be no purpose if life evolved from inanimate matter which only became animate by pure luck. Humankind's supposed 'cousins,' the monkey and apes are not bothered with questions of existence, so why should human beings be bothered with them?

Although most people put the question of why we are created aside after occasional brief reflection, it is extremely critical for human beings to know the answer. Without knowledge of the correct answer, human beings become indistinguishable from the other animals around them. The animal necessities and desires of eating, drinking and pro-creating become the purpose of human existence by default, and human effort is then focused in this limited sphere. When material satisfaction develops into the most important goal in life, human existence becomes even more degraded than that of the lowest of animals. Human beings will consistently misuse their God-given intelligence when they lack knowledge of their purpose of existence. The degraded human mind uses its abilities to create drugs and bombs and becomes engrossed in fornication, pornography, homosexuality, fortune-telling, suicide, etc. Without knowledge of the purpose of life, human existence loses all meaning and is consequently wasted, and the reward of an eternal life of happiness in the hereafter is

---

[1] This view was expressed in his book *The Republic through his well-known metaphor of the cave*, where the changing physical world is compared to shadows cast on the wall of a cave by graven images (*The New Encyclopaedia Britannica*, vol. 25, p. 552).

completely destroyed. Therefore, it is of the utmost importance that human beings correctly answer the question "Why are we here?"

Humans most often turn to other human beings like themselves for the answers. However, the only place that clear and precise answers to these questions can be found is in the books of divine revelation. It was necessary that God reveal the purpose to man through His prophets, because human beings are incapable of arriving at the correct answers by themselves. All of the prophets of God taught their followers the answers to the question "Why did God create man?"

Judeo-Christian Scriptures

A survey of the Bible leaves the honest seeker of truth lost. The Old Testament seems more concerned with laws and the history of early man and the Jewish people than with answering the vital question concerning humanity's creation.[2] In Genesis, God creates the world and Adam and Eve in six days and 'rests' from His work on the seventh.[3] Adam and Eve disobey God and are punished and their son Cain kills their other son Abel and goes to live in the land of Nod. And God was 'sorry' that he had made

---

[2] In Isaiah the Israelites are created for God's glory, "1 But now thus says the Lord, he who created you, O' Jacob, he who formed you, O' Israel: ... [6] 'I will say to the north, Give up, and to the south, Do not withhold; bring my sons from afar and my daughters from the end of the earth, [7] every one who is called by my name, whom I created for my glory, whom I formed and made.'" (Revised Standard Version, Isaiah 43:1, 6-7.)

[3] "2 And on the seventh day God finished his work which he had done, and he rested on the seventh day from all his work which he had done. 3 So God blessed the seventh day and hallowed it, because on it God rested from all his work which he had done in creation." (RSV, Genesis 2:2-3.)

man![4] Why are the answers not there in clear and unmistakable terms? Why is so much of the language symbolic, leaving the reader to guess at its meanings? For example, in Genesis 6:6 it is stated, "When men began to multiply on the face of the ground, and daughters were born to them, the sons of God saw that the daughters of men were fair; and they took to wife such of them as they chose." Who are these "sons of God"? Each Jewish sect and each of the many Christian sects who followed them have their own explanations. Which is the correct interpretation? The truth is that the purpose of man's creation was taught by the prophets of old, however, some of their followers — in collusion with the devils — later changed the scriptures. The answers became vague and much of the revelation was hidden in symbolic language. When God sent Jesus Christ to the Jews, he overturned the tables of those merchants who had set up businesses inside the temple,[5] and he preached against the ritualistic interpretation of the law practiced by the Jewish rabbis. He reaffirmed the law of Prophet Moses and revived it. He taught the purpose of life to his disciples and demonstrated how to fulfill it until his last moments in this world. However, after his departure from this world, his message was also distorted by some who claimed to be among his followers. The clear truth which he brought became vague, like the messages of the prophets before him. Symbolism was introduced, especially through the "Revelations" of John, and the Gospel which was revealed to Jesus was lost. Four other gospels composed by men were chosen by Athanasius, a fourth century bishop,[6] to replace the lost Gospel of Jesus Christ. And the 23

---

[4] "And the Lord was sorry that he had made man on the earth, and it grieved him to his heart." (RSV, Genesis 6:6.)

[5] Luke 19:45 (RSV).

[6] *The New Encyclopaedia Britannica*, vol. 14, p. 814.

books of writings of Paul and others included in the New Testament outnumbered even the four versions of the gospel.[7] As a result, New Testament readers cannot find precise answers to the question "Why did God create man?"[8] And one is forced to blindly follow the contrived dogmas of whatever sect they happen to belong to or adopt. The gospels are interpreted according to each sect's beliefs, and the seeker of truth is again left wondering, which one is correct?

The Incarnation of God

Perhaps the only common concept to most Christian sects regarding the purpose of mankind's creation is that God became man so that He could die at the hands of men to cleanse them of sin inherited from Adam and his descendants. According to them, this sin had become so great that no human act of atonement or repentance could erase it. God is so good that sinful man cannot stand before Him. Consequently, only God's sacrifice of Himself could save humankind from sin.

---

[7] In the mid-4th century manuscript called Codex Sinaiticus, the Letter of Barnabas and the Shepherd of Hermas are included as a part of the New Testament. (*The New Encyclopaedia Britannica*, vol. 14, p. 814.)

[8] What may be cited in the King James Version as the purpose of creation, Revelation 4:11 "Thou art worthy, O' Lord, to receive glory and honor and power: for thou hast created all things, and for thy pleasure they are and were created." is retranslated in the Revised Standard Version as: "Worthy art thou, our Lord and God, to receive glory and honour and power, for thou didst create all things, and by thy will they existed and were created." In Paul's letter to the Colossians he explains that the world was created for Jesus "15 He is the image of the invisible God, the first-born of all creation; 16 for in him all things were created, in heaven and on earth, visible and invisible, whether thrones or dominions or principalities or authorities — all things were created through him and for him." (RSV, Colossians 1:15.)

Belief in this man-made myth became the only source for salvation, according to the Church. Consequently, the Christian purpose of creation became the recognition of the 'divine sacrifice' and the acceptance of Jesus Christ as the Lord God. This may be deduced from the following words attributed to Jesus in the Gospel according to John, "For God so loved the world that he gave his only Son, that whoever believes in him should not perish but have eternal life." [9] However, if this is the purpose of creation and the prerequisite for everlasting life, why was it not taught by all the prophets? Why did God not become man in the time of Adam and his offspring so that all mankind would have an equal chance to fulfill their purpose for existence and attain everlasting life. Or did those before Jesus' time have another purpose for existence? All people today whom God has destined never to hear of Jesus also have no chance to fulfill their supposed purpose of creation. Such a purpose, is obviously too limited to fit the need of humankind.

Everything is God

The Hindu scriptures teach that there are many gods, incarnations of gods, persons of God and that everything is God, *Brahman*. In spite of the belief that the self (*atman*) of all living beings is actually *Brahman*, an oppressive caste system evolved in which the *Brahmans*, the priestly caste, possess spiritual supremacy by birth. They are the teachers of the *Vedas*[10] and

---

[9] John, 3:16 (RSV).

[10] The *Veda*, meaning "Knowledge," is a collective term for revealed (*sruti*; heard) sacred scriptures of the Hindus. All other works — in which the actual doctrines and practises of Hindus are encoded — are recognized as having being composed by human authors and are thus classed as *smriti* (remembered). (*The New Encyclopaedia Britannica*, vol. 20, p. 530.)

represent the ideal of ritual purity and social prestige. On the other hand, the *Sudra* caste are excluded from religious status and their sole duty in life is "to serve meekly"[11] the other three castes and their thousands of subcastes.

According to Hindu monist philosophers, humankind's purpose is the realization of their divinity and — following a path (*marga*) to emancipation (*moksha*) from the wheel of rebirth — the reabsorbtion of the human soul (*atman*) into the ultimate reality, *Brahman*. For those following the *bhakti* path,[12] the purpose is to love God because God created humankind to "enjoy a relationship — as a father enjoys his children" (*Srimad Bhagwatam*). For the ordinary Hindu, the main aim of worldly life lies in conforming to social and ritual duties, to the traditional rules of conduct for one's caste — the *karma* path.[13]

Although most of the religion of the Vedic texts, which revolves around rituals of fire sacrifice, has been eclipsed by Hindu doctrines and practices found in other texts, the absolute authority and sacredness of the *Veda* remains a central tenet of virtually all Hindu sects and traditions. The *Veda* is composed of four collections, the oldest of which is the *Rigveda* ("Wisdom of the Verses"). In these texts, God is described in the most confusing terms. The religion reflected in the *Rigveda* is a polytheism mainly concerned with appeasing deities associated with the sky and the atmosphere, the most important of which

---

[11] *Manava Dharmasastra* 1.91 (*The New Encyclopaedia Britannica*, vol. 20, p. 553.)

[12] The path of devotion to a personal God in which *murtis* (idols) are worshipped with the hope of going to *krishnaloka* (a spiritual planet) in their next lives.

[13] *The New Encyclopaedia Britannica*, vol. 20, p. 520.

were *Indra* (god of the heavens and rain), *Baruna* (guardian of the cosmic order), *Agni* (the sacrificial fire), and *Surya* (the Sun). In later Vedic texts, interest in the early Rigvedic gods declines, and polytheism begins to be replaced by a sacrificial pantheism to *Prajapati* ("Lord of Creatures"), who is the All. In the *Upanishads* (secret teachings concerning cosmic equations), *Prajapati* merges with the concept of *Brahman*, the supreme reality and substance of the universe, replacing any specific personification, thus transforming the mythology into abstract philosophy.[14] If the contents of these scriptures were all that human beings had to choose from for guidance, one would have to conclude that God hid both Himself and the purpose of creation from humankind.

God is not the author of confusion, nor does He wish difficulty for mankind. Consequently, when He revealed His final communication to humankind one thousand four hundred years ago, He ensured that it was perfectly preserved for all of the generations of human beings to come. In that final scripture, the Qur'an (Koran), God revealed His purpose for creating mankind and, through His last prophet, He clarified all of the details which man could comprehend. It is on the basis of this revelation and the prophetic explanations that we will analyze the precise answers to the question "Why did God create man?" in the coming pages.

---

[14] *The New Encyclopaedia Britannica*, vol. 20, Pp. 529-530.

WHY DID GOD CREATE?

From the point of view of God, an even more fundamental question needs to be asked, "Why did God create?" This question should be asked because humankind is not, in fact, the greatest creation. God says in Chapter *Ghâfir* of the final revelation:

﴿لَخَلْقُ ٱلسَّمَٰوَٰتِ وَٱلْأَرْضِ أَكْبَرُ مِنْ خَلْقِ ٱلنَّاسِ وَلَٰكِنَّ أَكْثَرَ ٱلنَّاسِ لَا يَعْلَمُونَ ﴿٥٧﴾﴾ (سورة غافر: ٥٧)

﴾Indeed, the creation of the heavens and the earth is greater than the creation of mankind, but most of mankind do not know it.﴿

(Qur'an 40: 57)

The composition of human beings is far less complex than the composition of the universe in which they exist. However, very few people reflect on this reality. Because of the apparent supremacy of human beings over the other creatures on this earth, man's journeys through space and the continued advancement of their technology and knowledge, humankind in every age becomes arrogant and considers itself the greatest thing in this world. It is worth noting that the majority of humankind's amazing discoveries are not concerning the human being, but his surroundings. Thus, human efforts tend to be focused on the material world rather than human beings. In this verse, God brings human beings back to their actual status in this world. Humankind is merely a small part of the existence which resulted from the miraculous act of divine creation. Thus, in order to understand why God created mankind, one first needs to answer the even more fundamental question of why God created.

The Creator

Creation is fundamentally the consequence of the divine attribute of being the Creator. A creator who does not create is something of a contradiction in terms. This is not to say that God needs His creation. God is free from all needs. It is creation which needs Him. But, as the greatness of a writer becomes apparent in his writings, the perfection of the divine creative attribute is manifest in creation. Creation in the true sense is unique to God alone. Although humans ascribe the act of creation to themselves, what they do is not true creation. Humankind merely manipulates what already exists—what was already created by God. A table is made from wood which came from trees and is held together with nails and screws made from metal that came from rocks. Human beings did not make the trees or the rocks. In fact, all human creations can be traced back to basic elements which humans cannot make. Even the artist 'creates' designs based on what he has seen. It is not possible to imagine what has not been perceived by the senses. Thus, all of the artist's thoughts are reflections on what was already created. Only God alone creates from nothing. This basic fact was and still is incomprehensible to some. Some ancient as well as modern philosophers, who could not comprehend how God could create from nothing, claimed that the created world and its contents are all originally a part of God.[1]

---

[1] This is also Hindu belief regarding the supreme reality, *Brahman*. In the last (10th) book of the *Rigveda*: in the "Hymn of the Cosmic Man" (*Purusasukta*),=

That is, according to them, God took a part of Himself and made the universe. This conclusion is based on comparing God to man, who can only 'create' by modifying what already exists. However, God denies any such comparisons which would give Him human limitations. In Chapter *ash-Shoorâ* of the final revelation, He states:

﴿...لَيْسَ كَمِثْلِهِۦ شَىْءٌ ۖ وَهُوَ ٱلسَّمِيعُ ٱلْبَصِيرُ ﴿١١﴾﴾ (سورة الشورى: ١١)

﴿... There is nothing like Him and He is the Hearing, the Seeing.﴾ *(Qur'an 42: 11)*

Thus, the act of creation is a consequence of the divine attribute of being the Creator. God describes Himself as the Creator in a variety of verses throughout the final revelation to emphasize to humankind that everything belongs to Him alone.

﴿ٱللَّهُ خَٰلِقُ كُلِّ شَىْءٍ ۖ وَهُوَ عَلَىٰ كُلِّ شَىْءٍ وَكِيلٌ ﴿٦٢﴾﴾ (سورة الزمر: ٦٢)

﴿Allah created all things and He is, over all things, Disposer of affairs.﴾ *(Qur'an 39: 62)*

﴿وَٱللَّهُ خَلَقَكُمْ وَمَا تَعْمَلُونَ ﴿٩٦﴾﴾ (سورة الصافات: ٩٦)

﴿And Allah created you and that which you do.﴾ *(Qur'an 37: 96)*

Man needs to realize that nothing takes place in this universe without the permission of God. To seek protection from

---

=it is said that the universe was created out of the parts of the body of a single cosmic man (*Purusa*) when his body was burned and dismembered at the primordial sacrifice. The four castes emerge from his body: the priest (*Brahman*) from the mouth, the warrior (*Rajanya*) from the arms, the peasant (*Vaisya*) from the thighs, and the servant (*Sudra*) from the legs. (*The New Encyclopaedia Britannica*, vol. 20, p. 531).

evil or to seek to acquire good from any source other than God is a major mistake. Due to ignorance, many people attempt to avoid misfortune and to gain good fortune through a variety of charms and amulets, astrology, palmistry, etc. Consequently, in the final revelation, Chapter *al-Falaq*, God informs human beings to seek refuge in God from evil:

﴿قُلْ أَعُوذُ بِرَبِّ ٱلْفَلَقِ ۝١ مِن شَرِّ مَا خَلَقَ ۝٢﴾ (سورة الفلق: ١-٢)

﴿Say: I seek refuge in the Lord of the dawn, from the evil of what He has created.﴾ *(Qur'an 113: 1-2)*

Allah, God Almighty, is not evil; He is good. He created a world in which evil or good can be done by beings to whom He gave this ability. However, no evil or good can take place in this world without the permission of God. This is why it is futile to turn to others besides God for help and protection.

﴿مَآ أَصَابَ مِن مُّصِيبَةٍ إِلَّا بِإِذْنِ ٱللَّهِ ... ۝١١﴾ (سورة التغابن: ١١)

﴿No calamity strikes except by Allah's permission﴾

(Qur'an 64: 11)

The final prophet of God, Muhammad (ﷺ), further elaborated on this concept, saying,

> "Be aware that if the whole of mankind gathered together to do something to help you, they would only be able to do something for you which Allah had already written for you. Likewise, if the whole of mankind gathered together to harm you, they would only be able to do something to harm you which Allah had already written to happen to you." [2]

---

[2] Reported by 'Abbâs and collected by Tirmidhi and authenticated in *Ṣaḥeeḥ Sunan at-Tirmidhi*, vol. 2, Pp. 308-9, hadith no. 2043.

The Merciful, The Forgiving

In the creation of humankind, the divine attributes of forgiveness, mercy and kindness are also manifested. Human beings were created good and pure with a natural awareness of good and evil. The Almighty also created desires in humans, and gave them an ability to control those desires according to divine law or to turn them loose and follow them blindly. God created mankind knowing that they would disobey Him. Consequently, He taught human beings, beginning with Adam, how to repent and thereby purify themselves of their sins. Adam and Eve represent a pattern for all mankind to follow. They forgot the commandment of God, and Satan played on their desires. After they had disobeyed God, they turned back to Him in repentance, and He forgave them. In humankind's disobedience and turning back to God in repentance, the divine attributes of total forgiveness and infinite mercy become manifest. The final Prophet (ﷺ) informed his followers of this reality, saying,

> "If you did not commit sins and turn to Allah, seeking His forgiveness, He would have replaced you with another people who would sin, ask Allah's forgiveness and He would forgive them."[3]

Every one of the 114 Chapters of the final revelation, except one, begins with the prayer, "In the name of Allah, the Beneficent the Most Merciful." Allah's attributes of mercy and forgiveness are stressed to encourage humans not to fall into despair. No matter how great the sins of human beings may be, God can forgive them if man turns back to Him in sincere repentance. The Messenger

---

[3] *Ṣaḥeeḥ Muslim*, vol. 4, Pp. 1435-6, hadith no. 6621, reported by Abu Ayyoob al-Anṣâri.

(ﷺ) was quoted as saying,

> "When Allah created the universe, He made an obligation on Himself (recorded) in a document kept by Him: My mercy supersedes my wrath." [4]

He was also reported to have said,

> "(Allah created) mercy with one hundred parts, one of which was sent down upon the jinn, human beings and other living beings. It is out of this one part that they love each other, show kindness to each other and even the animals treat their offspring with affection. Allah has reserved the remaining ninety-nine parts for His true worshippers on the Day of Resurrection."[5]

Had Allah wished, He could have created mankind like angels, incapable of committing sin. However, that was not His wish, as He had already created angels. Human beings were created capable of making mistakes and when they realize their errors and seek God's forgiveness, the divine attributes of mercy and forgiveness become manifest.

Supreme Justice

In the judgment of mankind at the end of this world, God's attributes of supreme justice and fairness also become manifest. Based on His infinite knowledge, God could have created all members of the human race who were to live on earth and immediately placed some of them in paradise and the remainder in hell. Before creating man, Allah already knew what choices they

---

[4] *Ṣaḥeeḥ Muslim*, vol. 4, p. 1437, hadith no. 6628, reported by Abu Hurayrah.
[5] Ibid., vol. 4, p. 1437, hadith no. 6631, reported by Abu Hurayrah.

would make in this life, what provision and opportunities He would give them, and in what state of belief or disbelief they would die. Therefore, in one sense it could be said that some people were created for Paradise and others for Hell. 'Â'ishah (⁣), wife of the Prophet Muhammad (⁣), quoted him as saying,

"Don't you know that Allah created Paradise and Hell, and He created inhabitants for each?" [6]

If God had immediately placed those headed for Paradise in Paradise, they would not question God's decision. Those in Paradise would happily accept an everlasting life of bliss and be thankful that they were not placed in Hell. However, those immediately placed in Hell would ask why. They would feel a sense of unfairness due to their ignorance of what they would have done had they lived on earth. Those in Hell would relentlessly argue that had they been given a chance to live out their lives on earth, they would have believed and done righteous deeds. Consequently, Allah allows human beings to live out their lives on earth and make all the choices they would have made, so that everyone who enters hell will know that they chose hell by themselves. They will recognize God's mercy in their lives and acknowledge their sin in rejecting His signs and guidance. And they will accept His judgment as being just and beyond reproach. However, they will still beg for another chance to do good in this world, as God says in Chapter *as-Sajdah* of the Qur'an:

﴿وَلَوْ تَرَىٰ إِذِ ٱلْمُجْرِمُونَ نَاكِسُواْ رُءُوسِهِمْ عِندَ رَبِّهِمْ رَبَّنَآ أَبْصَرْنَا وَسَمِعْنَا فَٱرْجِعْنَا نَعْمَلْ صَٰلِحًا إِنَّا مُوقِنُونَ ۝﴾   (سورة السَّجدَة: ١٢)

---

[6] *Ṣaḥeeḥ Muslim*, vol. 4, p. 1400, hadith no. 6435.

﴿"If only you could see when the criminals are hanging their heads before their Lord, [saying], 'Our Lord! We have now seen and heard, so send us back and we will do righteous deeds. Verily, we now believe with certainty.'"﴾ *(Qur'an 32: 12)*

However, if Allah were to send them back to this world having forgotten what they had seen of hell, they would again choose evil and end up in hell as before. God spoke about this in Chapter *al-An'âm*,

﴿... وَلَوْ رُدُّوا۟ لَعَادُوا۟ لِمَا نُهُوا۟ عَنْهُ وَإِنَّهُمْ لَكَٰذِبُونَ ﴿٢٨﴾﴾ (سورة الأنعام: ٢٨)

﴿... But if they were returned [to this world], they would certainly go back to what was forbidden to them. Indeed they are liars.﴾ *(Qur'an 6: 28)*

Divine Love

God's love is manifest in beings brought into existence, whether believer or disbeliever, to enjoy life, if only for a brief moment. It is also realized in the creation of Paradise for those who choose righteousness over evil. Allah states in the final revelation that He loves those who do good *(Qur'an 5: 13)*, those who are just *(Qur'an 5: 42)*, those who are pious *(Qur'an 9: 4)*, those who are patient *(Qur'an 3: 146)*, those who put their trust in Him *(Qur'an 3: 159)*, those who frequently turn to Him in repentance and those who purify themselves *(Qur'an 2: 222)*. However, it is He who has defined for human beings through the scriptures and the prophets what is good, just and pious. Consequently, those who follow the prophets are most beloved to God. In Chapter *Âl 'Imrân,* Allah instructed Prophet Muhammad (ﷺ) to say the following to the believers:

﴿... إِن كُنتُمْ تُحِبُّونَ ٱللَّهَ فَٱتَّبِعُونِى يُحْبِبْكُمُ ٱللَّهُ وَيَغْفِرْ لَكُمْ ذُنُوبَكُمْ ... ﴿٣١﴾﴾ (سورة آل عمران: ٣١)

﴿... If you really love Allah, follow me and Allah will love you and forgive your sins...﴾ *(Qur'an 3: 31)*

The prophets should be followed not only in the compulsory acts ordained by God, but also in their eagerness to do acts of voluntary worship.

The love of God is also manifest in His mercy and blessings which He grants to those who deserve them as well as those who do not. But, it is particularly manifest in His willingness to forgive the sins of whomsoever turns to Him in sincere repentance. From the creation of Adam and Eve, repentance was granted to them to erase their sins as an example to all human beings who would follow them into this world. No matter how great human sins may become, the door for sincere repentance remains open until the last day of this world. Anas (رضي الله عنه) quoted Allah's Messenger (ﷺ) as saying,

> "Allah, the Almighty, has said, O' son of Adam, as long as you call on Me and ask of Me, I will forgive what you have done, and I do not mind. O' son of Adam, even if your sins reached the clouds and you asked My forgiveness, I will forgive you. O' son of Adam, if you came to Me with sins nearly as great as the earth and you met Me without giving Me partners, I will give you a similar amount of forgiveness." [7]

---

[7] Collected by Tirmidhi and authenticated in *Ṣaḥeeḥ Sunan at-Tirmidhi*, vol. 3, Pp. 175-6, hadith no. 2805.

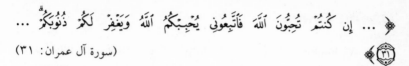

Divine Grace

As for those in Paradise, they will not enter it solely based on their good deeds. It is the grace of God which will ultimately carry them there. The final Prophet of Allah (ﷺ) said in this regard,

> "Try your best to do right, and be happy. For none will enter Paradise only because of his deeds."
>
> His Companions said, "O' Messenger of Allah! Not even you?"
>
> He replied, "Not even I, unless Allah envelops me in His mercy and grace."[8]
>
> And bear in mind that the deed most loved by Allah is one done constantly, even though it is small.[9]

However, God's grace is not arbitrary. It is based on both correct faith and righteous deeds. In Chapter *al An'âm*, Allah (ﷻ) says:

﴿مَن جَآءَ بِٱلْحَسَنَةِ فَلَهُۥ عَشْرُ أَمْثَالِهَا ۖ وَمَن جَآءَ بِٱلسَّيِّئَةِ فَلَا يُجْزَىٰٓ إِلَّا مِثْلَهَا وَهُمْ لَا يُظْلَمُونَ ﴿١٦٠﴾﴾ (سورة الأنعام: ١٦٠)

﴿Whoever brings a good deed, will have [the value of] ten like it, and whoever brings an evil deed will only be punished with one like it, and they will not be wronged.﴾ *(Qur'an 6: 160)*

Were God to hold humankind to account strictly, no one's good deeds would outweigh their evil deeds. However, God has manifested His grace by multiplying the value of good deeds,

---

[8] *Ṣaḥeeḥ Muslim*, vol. 4, p. 1473, hadith no. 6765, reported by Abu Hurayrah.

[9] Ibid., vol. 4, Pp. 1473-4, hadith no. 6770, reported by 'Â'ishah.

while keeping evil deeds at their face value. It is by the grace of God that the true believers enter Paradise. This does not mean that deeds have no role. Deeds have a major role, but they are not the deciding factor. God's grace outweighs them.

Consequently, the creation of human beings, the errors that they make and the good that they do are all circumstances for the manifestation of God's attributes of mercy and forgive-ness, His attribute of justice and His attribute of grace.

Humankind should not question why God chose to manifest His attributes in this way. It can only be assumed that this was the best way, because Allah describes Himself as being the Most Wise and the Most Knowledgeable. Humans can only understand what Allah chooses to reveal to them.

﴿... وَلَا يُحِيطُونَ بِشَيْءٍ مِّنْ عِلْمِهِۦٓ إِلَّا بِمَا شَآءَ ... ﴿٢٥٥﴾﴾

(سورة البَقَـرَة: ٢٥٥)

﴿They will only encompass of His knowledge what He wishes.﴾

(Qur'an 2: 255)

Thus, they should not try to equate themselves with God. If He has told humankind why He decided to do something, it is not for them to question why He decided to decide. Such questions are without end and thus beyond human scope. It is they who will be questioned on the Day of Judgment about their actions and intentions and not He. In Chapter *al-Anbiyâ'*, Allah (ﷻ) addresses this point:

﴿لَا يُسْـَٔلُ عَمَّا يَفْعَلُ وَهُمْ يُسْـَٔلُونَ ﴿٢٣﴾﴾ (سورة الأنبياء: ٢٣)

﴿He cannot be questioned as to what He does, while they will be questioned.﴾

(Qur'an 21: 23)

In this regard Prophet Muhammad (ﷺ) was reported by Ibn 'Abbâs to have said,

> "Reflect on the creation of Allah but do not reflect on Allah."[10]

To reflect on the reality of Allah is to reflect on the infinite. And, as the mind boggles when it reflects on the limits of the finite universe and the galaxies and stars within it, it will be more confounded when it attempts to understand the uncreated. The Prophet (ﷺ) warned that the Satanic forces would seek to introduce doubts in the hearts of the believers by raising unanswerable questions about God. Abu Hurayrah (رضي الله عنه) related that Allah's Messenger (ﷺ) said,

> "Satan will come to everyone of you and ask, 'Who created this and that?' — until he questions, 'Who created your Lord?' When he comes to that, one should seek refuge in Allah [say, I affirm my faith in Allah and His prophets][11] and avoid [such thoughts]."[12]

---

[10] Collected by Abu Nu'aym in *al-Hilyah* and authenticated by Shaykh al-Albâni in *Silsilat al-Aḥâdeeth aṣ-Ṣaḥeeḥah*, vol. 4, p. 12, hadith no. 1788. There is also a similar narration from Ibn 'Umar collected by aṭ-Ṭabarâni in *al-Awsaṭ* and al-Bayhaqi in *Shu'ab al-Eemân*.

[11] *Ṣaḥeeḥ Muslim*, vol. 1, p. 77, hadith nos. 242 & 243.

[12] Ibid., vol. 1, p. 77, hadith no. 244 and *Ṣaḥeeḥ al-Bukhari*, vol. 4, p. 320, hadith no. 496.

WHY DID GOD CREATE MANKIND?

FROM THE PERSPECTIVE OF HUMANKIND, THE QUESTION "Why did God create man?" implies "For what purpose was man created?" In the final revelation, this question is answered without any ambiguity. Humans are first informed by God that every human being is born with an innate consciousness of God. In Chapter *al-A'râf*, Allah (ﷻ) said:

﴿وَإِذْ أَخَذَ رَبُّكَ مِنۢ بَنِىٓ ءَادَمَ مِن ظُهُورِهِمْ ذُرِّيَّتَهُمْ وَأَشْهَدَهُمْ عَلَىٰٓ أَنفُسِهِمْ
أَلَسْتُ بِرَبِّكُمْ ۖ قَالُوا۟ بَلَىٰ ۛ شَهِدْنَآ ۛ أَن تَقُولُوا۟ يَوْمَ ٱلْقِيَٰمَةِ إِنَّا كُنَّا عَنْ هَٰذَا
غَٰفِلِينَ ﴿١٧٢﴾ أَوْ تَقُولُوٓا۟ إِنَّمَآ أَشْرَكَ ءَابَآؤُنَا مِن قَبْلُ وَكُنَّا ذُرِّيَّةً مِّنۢ بَعْدِهِمْ ۖ
أَفَتُهْلِكُنَا بِمَا فَعَلَ ٱلْمُبْطِلُونَ ﴿١٧٣﴾﴾ (سورة الأعراف: ١٧٢-١٧٣)

﴿[Remember] when your Lord extracted from the loins of Adam's children their descendants and made them testify [saying], 'Am I not your Lord?' They said, 'Yes, we testify to it.' [This was] in case you say on the Day of Judgment, 'We were unaware of this.' Or you say, 'It was our ancestors who worshipped others besides God and we are only their descendants. Will you then destroy us for what the falsifiers did?'﴾ *(Qur'an 7: 172-3)*

The Prophet (ﷺ) explained that,

> "When Allah created Adam, He took from him a covenant at a place called Na'mân on the 9th day[1] of the 12th month.

---

[1] Known as the day of *'Arafât.*

> He then extracted from Adam all of his descendants who would be born until the end of the world, generation after generation, and spread them out before Him to take a covenant from them also. He spoke to them, face to face, making them bear witness that He was their Lord.[2]

Consequently, every human being is responsible for belief in God, which is imprinted on each and every soul. It is based on this inborn belief that Allah defined the purpose of humankind's creation in Chapter *adh-Dhâriyât*:

﴿وَمَا خَلَقْتُ ٱلْجِنَّ وَٱلْإِنسَ إِلَّا لِيَعْبُدُونِ ٥٦﴾ (سورة الذّاريات: ٥٦)

﴿I have not created the jinn[3] and humankind except to worship Me.﴾ *(Qur'an 51: 56)*

Thus, the essential purpose for which humankind was created is the worship of God. However, the Almighty is not in need of human worship. He did not create human beings out of a need on His part. If not a single human worshipped God, it would not diminish His glory in any way, and if all of mankind worshipped Him, it would not increase His glory in any way. God is perfect. He Alone exists without any needs. All created beings have needs. Consequently, it is humankind that needs to worship God.

---

[2] Collected by Aḥmad and authenticated in *Silsilah al-Aḥâdeeth aṣ-Ṣaḥeeḥah*, vol. 4, p. 158, hadith no. 1623.

[3] The jinn are a class of invisible rational beings created by God from the elements of fire. They were endowed by God with free will, like mankind. Consequently, some of them are righteous believers and others are evil disbelievers. The evil among them are commonly called demons, evil spirits, devils, etc.

The Meaning of Worship

To understand why human beings need to worship God, one must first understand what is meant by the term 'worship.' The English term 'worship' comes from the Old English *weorthscipe* meaning 'honor.' Consequently, worship in the English language is defined as 'the performance of devotional acts in honor of a deity.'[4] According to this meaning, man is instructed to show gratitude to God by glorifying Him. In Chapter *an-Naṣr* of the final revelation, Allah (ﷻ) says:

﴿فَسَبِّحْ بِحَمْدِ رَبِّكَ ... ﴾ (سورة النصر: ٣)

﴾Exalt [Him] with the praise of your Lord...﴿ *(Qur'an 110: 3)*

In glorifying God, man chooses to be in harmony with the rest of creation which naturally glorifies its Creator. Allah addresses this phenomenon in many chapters of the Qur'an. For example, in Chapter *al-Isrâ*, Allah states:

﴿تُسَبِّحُ لَهُ ٱلسَّمَٰوَٰتُ ٱلسَّبْعُ وَٱلْأَرْضُ وَمَن فِيهِنَّ وَإِن مِّن شَيْءٍ إِلَّا يُسَبِّحُ بِحَمْدِهِ وَلَٰكِن لَّا تَفْقَهُونَ تَسْبِيحَهُمْ ... ﴾ (سورة الاسراء: ٤٤)

﴾The seven heavens and the earth and whatever is in them glorify Him and there is nothing which does not glorify His praise.[5] However, you do not understand their way of glorification...﴿ *(Qur'an 17: 44)*

However, in Arabic, the language of the final revelation, worship is called *'ibâdah*, which is closely related to the noun

---

[4] *The Living Webster Encyclopedic Dictionary*, p. 1148.

[5] The thunder is described as glorifying God in (Qur'an 13: 13), the day and night in (Qur'an 21: 20) and the mountains in (Qur'an 38: 18).

'abd, meaning 'a slave.' A slave is one who is expected to do whatever his master wills. Consequently, worship, according to the final revelation, means 'obedient submission to the will of God.' This was the essence of the message of all the prophets sent by God to humankind. For example, this understanding of worship was emphatically expressed by Prophet Jesus in the Gospel according to Matthew, 7:21, "None of those who call me 'Lord' will enter the kingdom of God, but only the one who does the will of my Father in heaven." It should be noted that 'will' in this quote means 'what God wants human beings to do' and not 'what God permits humans to do,' because nothing happens in creation without the will (permission) of God. The 'Will of God' is contained in the divinely revealed laws which the prophets taught their followers. Consequently, obedience to divine law is the foundation of worship. In this sense, glorification also becomes worship when humans choose to obey God's instructions regarding His glorification.

The Need for Worship

Why do human beings need to worship and glorify God by obeying the divinely revealed laws? Because obedience to divine law is the key to success in this life and the next. The first human beings, Adam and Eve, were created in paradise and later expelled from paradise for disobeying the divine law. The only way for human beings to return to paradise is by obedience to the law. Jesus, the Messiah, was reported in the Gospel according to Matthew to have made obedience to the divine laws the key to paradise: Now behold, one came and said to him, "Good teacher, what good thing shall I do that I may have eternal life?" So he said to him, "Why do you call me good? No one is good but One, that is, God. But if you want to enter into life, keep the commandments."[6] Also in Matthew 5:19, Jesus Christ was reported to have insisted on strict obedience to the commandments, saying, "Whoever therefore breaks one of the least of these commandments, and teaches men so, shall be called least in the kingdom of heaven; but whoever does and teaches them, he shall be called great in the kingdom of heaven."

Divine laws represent guidance for humankind in all walks of life. They define right and wrong for them and offer human beings a complete system governing all of their affairs. The Creator alone knows best what is beneficial for His creation and what is not. The divine laws command and prohibit various acts and substances to protect the human spirit, the human body and human society from harm. In order for human beings to fulfill their potential by living righteous lives, they need to worship God through obedience to His commandments.

Remembrance of God

All of the various acts of worship contained in the divine laws are designed to help humans remember God. It is natural for human beings to sometimes forget even the most important things. Humans often become so engrossed in fulfilling their material needs that they totally forget their spiritual needs. Regular prayer is ordained to organize the day of the true believer around the remembrance of God. It interweaves spiritual needs with material needs on a daily basis. The regular daily need to eat, work and sleep is linked to the daily need to renew man's connection with God. With regard to regular prayer, Allah states

---

[6] Matthew 19:16-17 (RSV).

in the final revelation, Chapter *Ṭâhâ*:

﴿إِنَّنِيٓ أَنَا ٱللَّهُ لَآ إِلَٰهَ إِلَّآ أَنَا۠ فَٱعۡبُدۡنِي وَأَقِمِ ٱلصَّلَوٰةَ لِذِكۡرِيٓ ١٤﴾

(سورة طه: ١٤)

﴿Indeed, I am Allah, there is no deity except Me, so worship Me and establish regular prayer for My remembrance.﴾ *(Qur'an 20: 14)*

Regarding fasting, Allah (ﷻ) stated in Chapter *al-Baqarah*:

﴿يَٰٓأَيُّهَا ٱلَّذِينَ ءَامَنُواْ كُتِبَ عَلَيۡكُمُ ٱلصِّيَامُ كَمَا كُتِبَ عَلَى ٱلَّذِينَ مِن قَبۡلِكُمۡ لَعَلَّكُمۡ تَتَّقُونَ ١٨٣﴾ (سورة البقرة: ١٨٣)

﴿O' you who have believed, decreed upon you is fasting as it was decreed upon those before you that you may become righteous.﴾ *(Qur'an 2: 183)*

The believers are encouraged to remember God as much as possible. Although, moderation in all spheres of life, whether material or spiritual, is generally encouraged in divine law, an exception is made regarding the remembrance of Allah. It is virtually impossible to remember God too much. Consequently, in the final revelation, Chapter *al-Aḥzâb,* Allah encourages the believers to remember God as often as possible:

﴿يَٰٓأَيُّهَا ٱلَّذِينَ ءَامَنُواْ ٱذۡكُرُواْ ٱللَّهَ ذِكۡرٗا كَثِيرٗا ٤١﴾ (سورة الأحزاب: ٤١)

﴿O' believers! Remember Allah much.﴾ *(Qur'an 33: 41)*

Remembrance of God is stressed because sin is generally committed when God is forgotten. The forces of evil operate most freely when consciousness of God is lost. Consequently, the satanic forces seek to occupy people's minds with irrelevant thoughts and desires to make them forget God. Once God is forgotten, people willingly join the corrupt elements. The final revelation, the Qur'an, addresses this phenomenon in Chapter *al-Mujâdilah* as follows:

﴿ٱسْتَحْوَذَ عَلَيْهِمُ ٱلشَّيْطَٰنُ فَأَنسَىٰهُمْ ذِكْرَ ٱللَّهِ ۚ أُو۟لَٰٓئِكَ حِزْبُ ٱلشَّيْطَٰنِ ۚ أَلَآ إِنَّ حِزْبَ ٱلشَّيْطَٰنِ هُمُ ٱلْخَٰسِرُونَ ﴿١٩﴾﴾ (سورة المُجادلة: ١٩)

﴿Satan has overcome them and made them forget remembrance of Allah. Those are the party of Satan. Truly the party of Satan will be the losers.﴾ *(Qur'an 58: 19)*

God, through Divine law, has prohibited intoxicants and gambling primarily because they cause human beings to forget God. The human mind and body easily become addicted to drugs and games of chance. Once addicted, humankind's desire to continually be stimulated by them, leads them into all forms of corruption and violence among themselves. God says in Chapter *al-Mâ'idah* of the final revelation:

﴿إِنَّمَا يُرِيدُ ٱلشَّيْطَٰنُ أَن يُوقِعَ بَيْنَكُمُ ٱلْعَدَٰوَةَ وَٱلْبَغْضَآءَ فِى ٱلْخَمْرِ وَٱلْمَيْسِرِ وَيَصُدَّكُمْ عَن ذِكْرِ ٱللَّهِ وَعَنِ ٱلصَّلَوٰةِ ۖ فَهَلْ أَنتُم مُّنتَهُونَ ﴿٩١﴾﴾ (سورة المَائدة: ٩١)

﴿Satan's plan is to incite enmity and hatred among you with intoxicants and gambling, and hinder you from the remembrance of Allah and regular prayer. Will you not then abstain?﴾ *(Qur'an 5: 91)*

Consequently, humankind need to remember God for their own salvation and growth. All humans have times of weakness in which they commit sins. If they have no means of remembering God, they sink deeper and deeper into corruption with every sin. However, those who follow the divine laws will be constantly reminded of God, which will give them a chance to repent and correct themselves. The final revelation accurately describes this process in Chapter *Âl 'Imrân*:

﴿وَٱلَّذِينَ إِذَا فَعَلُوا۟ فَـٰحِشَةً أَوْ ظَلَمُوٓا۟ أَنفُسَهُمْ ذَكَرُوا۟ ٱللَّهَ فَٱسْتَغْفَرُوا۟ لِذُنُوبِهِمْ ... ﴿١٣٥﴾﴾ (سورة آل عمران: ١٣٥)

﴾Those who, when they commit an immorality or wrong themselves, remember Allah and seek forgiveness for their sins...﴿ *(Qur'an 3: 135)*

The Religion of Islam

The most complete system of worship available to human beings today is the system found in the religion of Islam. The very name 'Islam' means 'submission to the will of God.' Although it is commonly referred to as 'the third of the three monotheistic faiths,' it is not a new religion at all. It is the religion brought by all of the prophets of God for humankind. Islam was the religion of Adam, Abraham, Moses and Jesus. God addresses this issue in the final revelation with regard to Prophet Abraham, saying:

﴿مَا كَانَ إِبْرَٰهِيمُ يَهُودِيًّا وَلَا نَصْرَانِيًّا وَلَـٰكِن كَانَ حَنِيفًا مُّسْلِمًا وَمَا كَانَ مِنَ ٱلْمُشْرِكِينَ ﴿٦٧﴾﴾ (سورة آل عمران: ٦٧)

﴾Abraham was neither a Jew nor a Christian, but he was an upright Muslim who was not of the polytheists.﴿ *(Qur'an 3: 67)*

Since there is only One God, and humankind are one species, the religion which God has ordained for human beings is one. He did not prescribe one religion for the Jews, another for Indians, yet another for Europeans, etc. Human spiritual and social needs are uniform, and human nature has not changed since the first man and woman were created. Consequently, no other religion is acceptable to God besides Islam, as He clearly states in Chapter *Âl 'Imrân* of the final revelation:

﴿إِنَّ ٱلدِّينَ عِندَ ٱللَّهِ ٱلْإِسْلَٰمُ ... ﴿١٩﴾﴾ (سورة آل عِمرَان: ١٩)

﴿Indeed, the religion in the sight of Allah is Islam...﴾

(Qur'an 3: 19)

﴿وَمَن يَبْتَغِ غَيْرَ ٱلْإِسْلَٰمِ دِينًا فَلَن يُقْبَلَ مِنْهُ وَهُوَ فِى ٱلْءَاخِرَةِ مِنَ ٱلْخَٰسِرِينَ ﴿٨٥﴾﴾ (سورة آل عمران: ٨٥)

﴿And whoever desires a religion other than Islam will not have it accepted, and he will be among the losers in the hereafter.﴾

(Qur'an 3: 85)

Every Act Is Worship

In the Islamic system, each and every human act can be transformed into an act of worship. In fact, God commands the believers to dedicate their whole lives to Him. In Chapter *al-An'âm*, Allah (ﷻ) says:

﴿قُلْ إِنَّ صَلَاتِى وَنُسُكِى وَمَحْيَاىَ وَمَمَاتِى لِلَّهِ رَبِّ ٱلْعَٰلَمِينَ ﴿١٦٢﴾﴾

(سورة الأنعام: ١٦٢)

﴿Say, 'Surely my prayer, my sacrifice, my living and my dying are for Allah, Lord of the worlds.'﴾ *(Qur'an 6: 162)*

However, for that dedication to be acceptable to Allah, each act must fulfill two basic conditions:

1) **First, the act must be done sincerely for** the pleasure of God and not for the recognition and praise of human beings. The believer also has to be conscious of God while doing the deed

to insure that it is not something forbidden by Allah or the last Messenger (ﷺ).

In order to facilitate this transformation of mundane deeds into worship, Allah instructed the last Prophet (ﷺ) to prescribe short prayers to be said before even the simplest of acts. The shortest prayer which may be used for any circumstance is: *Bismillâh* (In the name of Allah). There are, however, many other prayers prescribed for specific occasions. For example, whenever a new piece of clothing is worn, the Prophet (ﷺ) taught his followers to say:

اللَّهُمَّ لَكَ الْحَمْدُ أَنْتَ كَسَوْتَنِيهِ، أَسْأَلُكَ مِنْ خَيْرِهِ وَخَيْرِ مَا صُنِعَ لَهُ، وَأَعُوذُ بِكَ مِنْ شَرِّهِ وَشَرِّ مَا صُنِعَ لَهُ.

"O' Allah, praise is due to You, for it is You Who has clothed me. I ask You for its benefit and the benefit for which it was made, and seek refuge in You from its evil and the evil for which it was made."[7]

2) The second condition is that the act be done in accordance with the prophetic way, called in Arabic the Sunnah. All of the prophets instructed their followers to follow their way because they were guided by God. What they taught were divinely revealed truths, and only those who followed their way and accepted the truths would inherit eternal life in paradise. It is in this context that Prophet Jesus, may the peace and blessings of God be upon him, was reported in the Gospel according to John 14:6, as saying, "I am the way, the truth, and the life: no man cometh unto the Father, but by me." Similarly, 'Abdullâh ibn

---

[7] *Sunan Abu Dawood*, vol. 3, p. 1125, hadith no. 4009 and authenticated in *Ṣaḥeeḥ Sunan Abu Dawood*, vol. 2, p. 760, hadith no. 3393.

Mas'ood related that one day Prophet Muhammad (ﷺ) drew a line in the dust for them and said,

> "This is Allah's path." He then drew several lines (branching off) to the right and to the left and said, "These are the paths [of misguidance] on each of which is a devil inviting people to follow it." He then recited the verse: ﴾Verily, this is my path, leading straight, so follow it. And do not follow [other] paths for they will scatter you about from Allah's path. That is His command to you in order that you may become righteous.﴿[8]"[9]

Thus, the only acceptable way to worship God is according to the way of the prophets. That being the case, innovation in religious affairs would be considered by God among the worst of all evils. Prophet Muhammad (ﷺ) was reported to have said,

> "The worst of all affairs is innovation in religion, for every religious innovation is a cursed, misleading innovation leading to the hellfire."[10]

Innovation in the religion is forbidden and unacceptable to God. The Prophet (ﷺ) was also reported by his wife, 'Â'ishah (رضي الله عنها), to have said,

> "He who innovates something in this matter of ours, that is not of it, will have it rejected."[11]

It is fundamentally due to innovations that the messages of the

---

[8] *Soorah al-An'âm* (6):153.

[9] Collected by Aḥmad, Nasâ'i and ad-Dârimi, and authenticated by Aḥmad Shâkir in *al-Musnad*, vol. 6, Pp. 89-90, hadith no. 4142.

[10] *Ṣaḥeeḥ Muslim*, vol. 2, p. 410, hadith no. 1885.

[11] *Ṣaḥeeḥ al-Bukhari*, vol. 3, Pp. 535-6, hadith no. 861, and *Ṣaḥeeḥ Muslim*, vol. 3, p. 931, hadith no. 4266.

earlier prophets were distorted and the many false religions in existence today evolved. The general rule to follow in order to avoid innovation in religion is that all forms of worship are prohibited, except those which have been specifically prescribed by God and conveyed to humans by the true messengers of God.

The Best of Creation

Those who believe in One Unique God, without partners or offspring, and do righteous deeds (according to the above-mentioned principles) become the crown of creation. That is, although humankind is not the greatest creation of Allah, they have the potential to become the best of His creation. In Chapter *al-Bayinah,* Allah states this fact as follows:

﴿إِنَّ ٱلَّذِينَ ءَامَنُوا۟ وَعَمِلُوا۟ ٱلصَّٰلِحَٰتِ أُو۟لَٰٓئِكَ هُمْ خَيْرُ ٱلْبَرِيَّةِ ۝٧﴾

(سورة البيّنة : ٧)

﴿Surely, those who believe and do righteous deeds are the best of creation.﴾ *(Qur'an 98: 7)*

The Gravest Sin

To contradict the purpose of one's creation is then the greatest evil that a human being can commit. 'Abdullâh reported that he asked Allah's Messenger (ﷺ) which sin is the gravest in Allah's sight and he replied,

"To give Allah a partner, even though He created you."[12]

Worshipping others besides God, called *shirk* in Arabic, is the

---

[12] *Ṣaḥeeḥ Muslim*, vol. 1, Pp. 50-1, hadith no. 156.

only unforgivable sin. If a human being dies without repenting from his or her sins, Allah may forgive all their sins except *shirk*. In this regard, God stated the following in Chapter *an-Nisâ'*:

﴿إِنَّ ٱللَّهَ لَا يَغْفِرُ أَن يُشْرَكَ بِهِۦ وَيَغْفِرُ مَا دُونَ ذَٰلِكَ لِمَن يَشَآءُ ... ﴿٤٨﴾﴾

(سورة النِّسَاء: ٤٨)

﴿Surely Allah will not forgive the worship of others besides Him, but He forgives sins less than that to whomever He wishes...﴾

(Qur'an 4: 48)

Worshipping others besides God essentially involves giving the attributes of the Creator to His creation. Each sect or religion does this in their own particular way. A small but very vocal group of people down through the ages have actually denied God's existence.[13] To justify their rejection of the Creator, they were obliged to make the illogical claim that this world has no beginning. Their claim is illogical because all of the observable parts of the world have beginnings in time, therefore it is only reasonable to expect the sum of the parts to also have a beginning. It is also only logical to assume that whatever caused the world to come into existence could not have been a part of the world nor could it have a beginning like the world. The atheist assertion that

---

[13] *Hinayana* Buddhism (400-250 BC), the earlier and more strict of the two interpretations of Buddhism which arose after Gautama Buddha's death, clearly states that there is no God. Jainism as systematized by Vardhamana also asserts that there is no God, but liberated souls, according to the teachings, attain immortality and omniscience. In the 19th and 20th centuries a number of European philosophers proclaimed what came to be known as the "death of God philosophy." The German philosopher, Philipp Mainlander (1841-1876), the Prussian, Friedrich Nietzsche (1844-1900), the Frenchman, Jean Paul Sartre (1905-1980) all argued the non-existence of God. (*Dictionary of Philosophy and Religion*, Pp. 72, 262-3, 327 and 508-9).

the world has no beginning means that the matter which makes up the universe is eternal. This is a statement of shirk, whereby God's attribute of being without beginning is given to His creation. The numbers of genuine atheists have historically always been quite small because, in spite of their claims, they instinctively know that God does exist. That is, in spite of decades of communist indoctrination, the majority of Russians and Chinese continued to believe in God. The Almighty Creator pointed out this phenomenon in Chapter *an-Naml,* saying:

﴿وَجَحَدُوا بِهَا وَاسْتَيْقَنَتْهَا أَنفُسُهُمْ ظُلْمًا وَعُلُوًّا ... ﴿١٤﴾﴾ (سورة النمل: ١٤)

﴿And they denied [the signs] wrongfully and arrogantly, though within themselves they were convinced of them...﴾ *(Qur'an 27: 14)*

To atheists and materialists, life has no purpose beyond the fulfillment of their desires. Consequently, their desires also become the god which they obey and submit to instead of the One True God. In Chapter *al-Furqân* of the final revelation, Allah said:

﴿أَرَأَيْتَ مَنِ اتَّخَذَ إِلَٰهَهُ هَوَاهُ ... ﴿٤٣﴾﴾ (سورة الفرقان: ٤٣)

﴿Have you seen the one who takes his desires as his god his own desire?...﴾ *(Qur'an 25: 43)*

Christians gave Prophet Jesus Christ the attributes of the Creator by first making him co-eternal with God,[14] then by making him a personality of God whom they titled 'God the Son.' Hindus, on the other hand, believe that God has become man in many ages, by incarnations called *avatars,* and then they divided

---

[14] John 1:1 & 14 "**1** In the beginning was the Word, and the Word was with God, and the Word was God.... **14** And the Word became flesh and dwelt among us, full of grace and truth;" (RSV).

God's attributes between three gods, *Brahma* the creator, *Vishnu* the preserver and *Shiva* the destroyer.

Love of God

Shirk also occurs when human beings love, trust or fear the creation more than Allah. In Chapter *al-Baqarah* of the last revelation, God said:

﴿وَمِنَ ٱلنَّاسِ مَن يَتَّخِذُ مِن دُونِ ٱللَّهِ أَندَادًا يُحِبُّونَهُمْ كَحُبِّ ٱللَّهِ ۖ وَٱلَّذِينَ
ءَامَنُوٓا۟ أَشَدُّ حُبًّا لِّلَّهِ ... ﴿١٦٥﴾﴾ (سورة البقرة: ١٦٥)

﴿There are among men those who worship others besides Allah as equals to Him. They love them as only Allah should be loved. But those who believe have a stronger love for Allah...﴾ *(Qur'an 2: 165)*

When these and other similar emotions are directed more strongly to the creation, they cause human beings to disobey God in an effort to please other humans. However, only Allah deserves a complete human emotional commitment, for it is He, alone, who should be loved and feared over all creation. Anas ibn Mâlik (رضي الله عنه) narrated that the Prophet (ﷺ) said,

> "Whoever possesses (the following) three characteristics has tasted the sweetness of faith: he who loves Allah and His Messenger above all else; he who loves another human being for Allah's sake alone; and he who hates to return to disbelief after Allah has rescued him as he hates to be thrown into a fire."[15]

All the reasons for which humans love other humans or love other created beings are reasons to love God more than His

[15] *Ṣaḥeeḥ Muslim*, vol. 1, p. 30, hadith no. 67.

creation. Humans love life and success, and dislike death and failure. Since Allah is the ultimate source of life and success, He deserves the full love and devotion of humankind. Humans also love those who benefit them and help them when they are in need. Since all benefit *(Qur'an 7: 188)* and help *(Qur'an 3: 126)* come from God, He should be loved above all else.

﴿... وَإِن تَعُدُّوا نِعْمَتَ اللَّهِ لَا تُحْصُوهَا ... ﴿٣٤﴾﴾ (سورة إبراهيم: ٣٤)

﴿... If you try to count Allah's blessings, you will not be able to add them up...﴾ *(Qur'an 14: 34)*

However, the supreme love which humans should feel for God must not be reduced to the common denominator of their emotional love for creation. Just as the love humans feel for animals should not be the same as what they feel for other humans,[16] the love of Allah should transcend the love humans feel towards one another. Human love of God should be, fundamentally, a love manifest in complete obedience to the laws of God, as stated in Chapter *Âl 'Imrân*, ﴿If you love Allah, then follow me [the Prophet] and Allah will love you.﴾[17] This is not an abstract concept, because human love of other humans also implies obedience. That is, if a loved one requests that something be done, humans will strive to do it according to the level of their love for that person.

The love of God should also be expressed in the love of those whom God loves. It is inconceivable that one who loves Allah could hate those whom Allah loves and love those whom

---

16 The huge sums of money currently being spent protecting endangered species of animals while humans are left to starve and die of disease is among the major crimes of the 20th century.

17 (Qur'an 3: 31).

He hates. The Prophet (ﷺ) was quoted by Abu Umâmah as saying,

> "He who loves for Allah and hates for Allah, gives for Allah and withholds for Allah, has perfected his faith."[18]

Consequently, those whose faith is proper will love all those who love God. In Chapter Maryam, Allah indicates that He puts love in the hearts of the believers for those who are righteous.

﴿إِنَّ ٱلَّذِينَ ءَامَنُوا۟ وَعَمِلُوا۟ ٱلصَّٰلِحَٰتِ سَيَجْعَلُ لَهُمُ ٱلرَّحْمَٰنُ وُدًّا ﴿٩٦﴾﴾

(سورة مريم: ٩٦)

﴿Surely, Allah the Most-Merciful will bestow love [in the hearts of] those who believe and do righteous deeds.﴾ *(Qur'an 19: 96)*

Abu Hurayrah (رضي الله عنه) also related that Allah's Messenger (ﷺ) said the following in this regard,

> "If Allah loves a servant He informs angel Gabriel that He loves So-and-so and tells him to love him, so Gabriel loves him. Then Gabriel calls out to the inhabitants of the heavens, 'Allah loves So-and-so, therefore love him.' So the inhabitants of the heavens love him. Then he is granted the love of the people of the earth."[19]

---

[18] Collected by Aḥmad, Tirmidhi and Abu Dawood (*Sunan Abu Dawood*, vol. 3, p. 1312, hadith no. 3664, and authenticated in *Ṣaḥeeḥ Sunan Abu Dawood*, vol. 3, p. 886, hadith no. 3915).

[19] *Ṣaḥeeḥ al-Bukhari*, vol. 4, p. 291, hadith no. 431, and *Ṣaḥeeḥ Muslim*, vol. 4, p. 1385, hadith no. 6373.

Prayers

Prayers should only be directed to God alone, for only He can answer prayers. He is accessible as long as He is called upon sincerely.

﴿وَإِذَا سَأَلَكَ عِبَادِي عَنِّي فَإِنِّي قَرِيبٌ ۖ أُجِيبُ دَعْوَةَ الدَّاعِ إِذَا دَعَانِ ... ﴿١٨٦﴾﴾

(سورة البقرة: ١٨٦)

﴾When My servants ask you [O' Muhammad] about Me, [tell them] that I am near, I respond to the invocation of the supplicant when he calls upon Me...﴿ *(Qur'an 2: 186)*

The Prophet (ﷺ) emphasized this point, saying,

> "If you ask in prayer, ask only Allah, and if you seek help, seek it only from Allah."[20]

Thus, prayer to human beings or through human beings, dead or living, is a form of shirk. The one to whom prayers are directed becomes an object of worship. An-Nu'mân ibn Basheer (رضي الله عنه) reported that the Prophet (ﷺ) said, "Supplication is worship."[21]

﴿إِنَّ الَّذِينَ تَدْعُونَ مِن دُونِ اللَّهِ عِبَادٌ أَمْثَالُكُمْ ... ﴿١٩٤﴾﴾

(سورة الأعراف: ١٩٤)

﴾Indeed, those you [polytheists] call upon besides Allah are servants like you...﴿ *(Qur'an 7: 194)*

[20] Reported by Ibn 'Abbâs and collected by Tirmidhi and authenticated in *Ṣaḥeeḥ Sunan at-Tirmidhi*, vol. 2, Pp. 308-9, hadith no. 2043. See *an-Nawawi's Forty Hadith*, p. 68, no. 19 and *Mishkat al-Maṣâbeeḥ*, vol. 2, p. 1099.

[21] *Sunan Abu Dawood*, vol. 1, p. 387, hadith no. 1474 and authenticated in *Ṣaḥeeḥ Sunan Abu Dawood*, vol. 1, p. 277, hadith no. 1312.

Thus, the Catholic Christian practice of praying to saints is *shirk.* If something is lost, Saint Anthony of Thebes is prayed to in order to help find it.[22] St. Jude Thaddaeus is the patron saint of the impossible and is prayed to for intercession in incurable illnesses, unlikely marriages or the like.[23] And it used to be that when someone set out on a journey, Saint Christopher, the patron saint of travelers, was the object of prayers for protection. However, in 1969 St. Christopher was unceremoniously struck off the list of saints by papal decree, after it was confirmed that he was fictitious.[24] Prayers to Mary, the mother of Jesus, and to the angels, as on Michaelmas[25] are also *shirk.* Even Christians who shun saint worship commit *shirk* whenever they direct prayers to Prophet Jesus, through him or in his name. Likewise, any Muslim who prays to Prophet Muhammad (ﷺ) commits *shirk.* Consequently, God commanded the Prophet (ﷺ) to inform his followers as follows in Chapter *al-A'râf*:

﴿قُل لَّآ أَمۡلِكُ لِنَفۡسِي نَفۡعٗا وَلَا ضَرًّا إِلَّا مَا شَآءَ ٱللَّهُۚ وَلَوۡ كُنتُ أَعۡلَمُ ٱلۡغَيۡبَ
لَٱسۡتَكۡثَرۡتُ مِنَ ٱلۡخَيۡرِ وَمَا مَسَّنِيَ ٱلسُّوٓءُۚ ... ﴿١٨٨﴾﴾ (سورة الأعراف: ١٨٨)

﴿Say, 'I hold not for myself [the power of] benefit or harm, except what Allah has willed. And if I knew the unseen, I could have acquitted much wealth, and no harm would have touched me...'﴾

(Qur'an 7: 188)

---

[22] *The World Book Encyclopaedia*, vol. 1, p. 509.

[23] Ibid., vol. 11, p. 146.

[24] Ibid., vol. 3, p. 417.

[25] The Christian feast of St. Michael the Archangel, celebrated in the western churches on September 29 and in the Eastern (Orthodox) Church on November 8. In the Roman Catholic Church, it is the Feast of SS. Michael, Gabriel, and Raphael, archangels; in the Anglican Church, its proper name is the Feast of St. Michael and All Angels (*The New Encyclopaedia Britannica*, vol. 8, p. 95).

Abu Hurayrah reported that when the verse, "﴾Warn your nearest relatives,﴿[26] was revealed to the Prophet, he (ﷺ) said the following to his relatives:

> "O' people of Quraysh, secure deliverance from Allah (by doing good deeds), for I cannot avail you at all against Allah... O' Fâṭimah, daughter of Muhammad, ask me whatever you wish [in this life], but I have nothing which can avail you against Allah."[27]

---

[26] *Soorah ash-Shoorâ* (26): 214.

[27] *Ṣaḥeeḥ al-Bukhari*, vol. 4, Pp. 478-9, hadith nos. 727 & 728, and *Ṣaḥeeḥ Muslim*, vol. 1, p. 136, hadith no. 402.

WHY DID GOD CREATE MANKIND ON EARTH?

The question concerning the purpose of mankind's creation may be expanded to include the world in which they live. The question would then be, "Why did God create human beings in this world?" Again, the answer to this question can easily be found in the final revelation, Chapters *al-Mulk* and *al-Kahf*:

﴿ٱلَّذِى خَلَقَ ٱلْمَوْتَ وَٱلْحَيَوٰةَ لِيَبْلُوَكُمْ أَيُّكُمْ أَحْسَنُ عَمَلًا ۚ وَهُوَ ٱلْعَزِيزُ ٱلْغَفُورُ ﴿٢﴾﴾

(سورة المُلك: ٢)

﴿[It is He] Who created death and life to test which of you is best in conduct; and He is the Mighty, the Forgiving.﴾ *(Qur'an 67: 2)*

﴿إِنَّا جَعَلْنَا مَا عَلَى ٱلْأَرْضِ زِينَةً لَّهَا لِنَبْلُوَهُمْ أَيُّهُمْ أَحْسَنُ عَمَلًا ﴿٧﴾﴾

(سورة الكهف: ٧)

﴿Surely We[1] have made all that is on the earth adornment for it that We may test which of them is best in deed.﴾ *(Qur'an 18: 7)*

Thus, the purpose for the creation of human beings in this world is to test their conduct.[2] This world of life and death, wealth

---

[1] "We" in the original Arabic is the majestic 'we,' referring to God.

[2] See also Chapter Hood (11):7.

and poverty, sickness and health, was created to sift out the righteous souls from the evil souls. Human conduct in this world is the measure of faith.

It should be noted, however, that the tests of conduct are not to inform God about humankind, for He knew everything there was to know about them before He created them. The tests serve to confirm on the Day of Judgment that those going to hell deserve it and those going to paradise only got there by God's grace. With regard to human beings in this life, the test of conduct serves two basic purposes: one, human spiritual growth, and the other, punishment or reward.

Spiritual Growth

The tests of this world are primarily for the spiritual growth of human beings. Just as an intense fire separates pure gold from the rough ore to which it is bound in nature, tests purify the moral character of the believers. They force the believers to choose their higher spiritual qualities over their lower desires. Although not every test is passed, even in failure the believer grows by learning spiritual lessons to help him or her in future tests.

Generosity and Contentment

For example, in all human societies the qualities of generosity and contentment are considered among the most noble characteristics. However, neither of these traits can develop if everyone has the same amount of wealth. Generosity can only be acquired when the human soul — aware that sharing with the needy is good — struggles against its desire to hoard its possessions. On the other hand, contentment is produced when the soul defeats the evils of envy and greed. The Creator wisely sets the stage for these spiritual struggles by unequally distributing wealth in this world. In Chapter *an-Naḥl* of the final revelation, Allah (ﷻ) says:

﴿وَٱللَّهُ فَضَّلَ بَعۡضَكُمۡ عَلَىٰ بَعۡضٖ فِي ٱلرِّزۡقِۚ ... ﴿٧١﴾﴾ (سورة النّحل: ٧١)

﴾Allah has favored some of you over others in sustenance...﴿ *(Qur'an 16: 71)*

Greed and stinginess are corrupt forms of the natural human desire to possess. The believers are informed by revelation that wealth is a trust given to humankind by God. Possessions exist in the world before humans are born and remain there after they die. If wealth is used according to divine instructions, it benefits those who have it in both worlds. But if it is used selfishly, it becomes a curse in this life and a cause for punishment in the next. In Chapter *al-Anfâl* of the final revelation, God warns the believers to beware of the dangers of wealth and children:

﴿وَٱعۡلَمُوٓاْ أَنَّمَآ أَمۡوَٰلُكُمۡ وَأَوۡلَٰدُكُمۡ فِتۡنَةٞ ... ﴿٢٨﴾﴾ (سورة الأنفال: ٢٨)

﴾Know that your property and children are but a trial...﴿ *(Qur'an 8: 28)*

God further warns the believers in Chapter *al-Munâfiqoon* (hypocrites) not to let their desire for wealth and children divert them from obedience to Him, for this is the test of possessions.

﴿يَٰٓأَيُّهَا ٱلَّذِينَ ءَامَنُواْ لَا تُلۡهِكُمۡ أَمۡوَٰلُكُمۡ وَلَآ أَوۡلَٰدُكُمۡ عَن ذِكۡرِ ٱللَّهِۚ ... ﴿٩﴾﴾ (سورة المنافقون: ٩)

﴾O' believers! Do not allow your wealth nor your children to divert you from the remembrance of Allah...﴿ *(Qur'an 63: 9)*

﴿... وَرَفَعَ بَعْضَكُمْ فَوْقَ بَعْضٍ دَرَجَٰتٍ لِّيَبْلُوَكُمْ فِي مَآ ءَاتَىٰكُمْ ... ﴿١٦٥﴾﴾

(سورة الأنعام: ١٦٥)

﴿... He raised some of you over others in rank to test you through what He granted you...﴾ *(Qur'an 6: 165)*

The desire to accumulate wealth cannot be satisfied in this life. The more human beings have, the more they want. The Prophet (ﷺ) stated,

> "If a man had a valley of gold, he would desire another, for nothing will fill his mouth but the dirt (of his grave). And Allah forgives whoever sincerely repents."[3]

This negative desire can only be overcome by giving of one's wealth charitably. Thus, Allah commanded the prophets to collect charity from the more wealthy among their followers for distribution among the poor.

﴿خُذْ مِنْ أَمْوَٰلِهِمْ صَدَقَةً تُطَهِّرُهُمْ وَتُزَكِّيهِم بِهَا ... ﴿١٠٣﴾﴾ (سورة التوبة: ١٠٣)

﴿Take from their wealth a charity by which you purify them and cause them increase...﴾ *(Qur'an 9: 103)*

Charity was institutionalized in Islam from its inception under the Arabic name, *Zakah*[4] (poor due or compulsory charity). Every believer with surplus wealth is obliged to give a set portion of it to the needy annually as an act of worship. To withhold *Zakah* is considered a major sin. Giving this charity helps the believers to realize that their wealth is not their own to do with as they please. It teaches them that they are only temporary

---

[3] *Ṣaḥeeḥ al-Bukhari*, vol. 8, Pp. 297-8, hadith no. 447.

[4] Literally *zakah* means 'purification' and 'growth'.

custodians of this wealth who must give a portion of it to those who are destitute. Consequently, God describes true believers as those who recognize the right of the needy to a portion of their wealth.

﴿وَفِيٓ أَمۡوَٰلِهِمۡ حَقّٞ لِّلسَّآئِلِ وَٱلۡمَحۡرُومِ ١٩﴾ (سورة الذاريات: ١٩)

﴾And in their wealth the beggars and needy have a right.﴿
(Qur'an 51: 19)

However, giving in charity should be done sincerely for the pleasure of God, and not for show or control of others. The reward for charity is completely lost when it is done for worldly gains. Allah addresses this reality in Chapter *al-Baqarah* as follows:

﴿يَٰٓأَيُّهَا ٱلَّذِينَ ءَامَنُواْ لَا تُبۡطِلُواْ صَدَقَٰتِكُم بِٱلۡمَنِّ وَٱلۡأَذَىٰ ... ٢٦٤﴾

(سورة البَقَرَة: ٢٦٤)

﴾O' you who have believed, do not invalidate your charities with reminders [of them] or injury...﴿ *(Qur'an 2: 264)*

Craving for wealth is further enhanced by envy. Consequently, God also instructed us not to desire what He has given others. God addresses this issue in Chapter *an-Nisâ'* of the final revelation as follows:

﴿وَلَا تَتَمَنَّوۡاْ مَا فَضَّلَ ٱللَّهُ بِهِۦ بَعۡضَكُمۡ عَلَىٰ بَعۡضٖۚ ... ٣٢﴾

(سورة النِّساء: ٣٢)

﴾Do not wish for that by which Allah has favored some of you over others...﴿ *(Qur'an 4: 32)*

The Prophet (ﷺ) reiterated this divine piece of advice, saying,

> "Look to those less fortunate than you, and do not look to those above you; it is better for you, in order that you do not deny what Allah has blessed you with."[5]

When human beings focus their attention on those who have more wealth than they do, envy begins to develop. They usually feel and express that God has been unfair to them. Ultimately, they may commit many sins to fulfill their desire for what others have. Instead, Islam advises them to consider those less fortunate than themselves. No matter how difficult circumstances may be, there are always others in more difficult situations. Consequently, reflecting on others less fortunate reminds human beings of the many bounties with which God has blessed them. It is in this spiritual struggle of avoiding envy that the higher quality of contentment develops. Furthermore, according to the teachings of the prophets, material possessions do not constitute the real wealth of this world. Abu Hurayrah (رضي الله عنه) quoted the last Messenger (ﷺ) as saying,

> "Wealth is not (measured) in property, but in contentment."[6]

Being content does not mean that human beings should accept whatever circumstance they find themselves in and not try to better themselves. It means that, after striving to do one's best to achieve a good standard of living, one should accept what Allah destines with a clear conscience. It is only by leaving one's affairs in the hands of God, after making an effort, that the hearts find rest from the desires for the pleasures of this world. In this regard, God states in Chapter *ar-Ra'd* of the final revelation:

---

[5] *Ṣaḥeeḥ al-Bukhari*, vol. 8, p. 328, hadith no. 497, and *Ṣaḥeeḥ Muslim*, vol. 4, p. 1530, hadith no. 7070.

[6] *Ṣaḥeeḥ al-Bukhari*, vol. 8, p. 304, hadith no. 453.

﴿... أَلَا بِذِكْرِ ٱللَّهِ تَطْمَئِنُّ ٱلْقُلُوبُ ﴿٢٨﴾﴾ (سورة الرّعد: ٢٨)

﴾... Indeed, it is by the remembrance of Allah that hearts find rest.﴿ *(Qur'an 13: 28)*

Calamities

Tests of this life also come in the form of 'misfortune' and calamities which contribute to the spiritual growth of the true believers and purify them of sin. Conversely, life's tests of misfortune remind errant believers to return to the correct path, and they punish disbelievers in this life before the next.

Patience

Calamities are the foundation on which the higher spiritual quality of patience is developed. Consequently, it is not surprising to find that the righteous are subject to many tragedies and difficulties in their lives. Sa'd (رضي الله عنه) reported that he asked the Prophet (ﷺ) who among mankind had the most trials, and he replied,

> "The prophets, then those most like them and then those most like them. Man is tested according to the level of his faith. If his faith is firm, his trials increase in severity, and if there is weakness in his faith, he will be tried accordingly."[7]

True patience is the product of complete trust in God at the time of calamity. Trust in one's Lord is an important aspect of worship and the natural consequence of real faith. Since belief in

---

[7] Collected by Tirmidhi and Ibn Mâjah and authenticated in *Ṣaḥeeḥ Sunan at-Tirmidhi*, vol. 2, p. 286, hadith no. 1956.

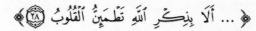

Allah means accepting that nothing takes place in the universe without His permission, then only Allah deserves humankind's complete trust. For, it is only God's promise which is never broken. No matter how righteous a human being may be, he or she is prone to error. Humans will always let one another down due to their erring nature. Consequently, Allah quotes Prophet Jacob in Chapter Yoosuf as saying:

﴿... إِنِ ٱلْحُكْمُ إِلَّا لِلَّهِ عَلَيْهِ تَوَكَّلْتُ وَعَلَيْهِ فَلْيَتَوَكَّلِ ٱلْمُتَوَكِّلُونَ ﴿٦٧﴾﴾

(سورة يُوسُف: ٦٧)

﴾... The decision is only for Allah; upon Him I have relied, and upon Him those who would rely [should] rely.﴿ *(Qur'an 12: 67)*

Allah further assures humankind that if they put their complete trust in Him, He will be sufficient for them in their most trying times.

﴿... وَمَن يَتَوَكَّلْ عَلَى ٱللَّهِ فَهُوَ حَسْبُهُۥٓ ... ﴿٣﴾﴾ (سورة الطَّلَاق: ٣)

﴾... Whoever relies on Allah, will find Him sufficient...﴿

(Qur'an 65: 3)

Trust in God is embodied in the firm belief that Allah Alone knows what is best for humankind; firm belief that what humans may perceive as being good for them may not, in the long run, be good for them. As Allah said in Chapter *al-Baqarah*:

﴿... وَعَسَىٰٓ أَن تَكْرَهُوا۟ شَيْـًٔا وَهُوَ خَيْرٌ لَّكُمْ ۖ وَعَسَىٰٓ أَن تُحِبُّوا۟ شَيْـًٔا وَهُوَ شَرٌّ لَّكُمْ ۗ وَٱللَّهُ يَعْلَمُ وَأَنتُمْ لَا تَعْلَمُونَ ﴿٢١٦﴾﴾ (سورة البقـرة: ٢١٦)

﴾... Perhaps you may dislike something when it is good for you, and you may like something when it is bad for you. Allah knows and you do not.﴿ *(Qur'an 2: 216)*

The trials by which Allah tests human beings are specifically tailored to their own individual needs and circumstances. God creates trials for each person according to their abilities in order to elicit the best in them. It would be unfair and unjust for human beings to be tried beyond their capacities and then be punished for their failures. Consequently, God emphasizes in many verses of the final revelation that He is not unfair to anyone. For example, He says in Chapter *al-Kahf*:

﴿... وَلَا يَظْلِمُ رَبُّكَ أَحَدًا ﴿٤٩﴾﴾ (سورة الكهف: ٤٩)

﴾... And your Lord does injustice to no one.﴿ *(Qur'an 18: 49)*

If Allah is truly just, it means that the trials human beings face in this life are not beyond their ability to handle. In order to reassure humankind, Allah states this fact repeatedly in the Qur'an. An example of His reassurance may be found in the second chapter, entitled *al-Baqarah*:

﴿لَا يُكَلِّفُ ٱللَّهُ نَفْسًا إِلَّا وُسْعَهَا ... ﴿٢٨٦﴾﴾ (سورة البَقَـرَة: ٢٨٦)

﴾Allah does not burden a soul beyond its capacity...﴿

(Qur'an 2: 286)

Furthermore, the Almighty promises that the difficult situations which humans face in life will not be without intervals of rest. If trials were continuous they would certainly become unbearable. Consequently, every test is followed by a period of relief, as Allah emphatically states twice in Chapter *al-Inshirâḥ* (or *ash-Sharḥ*):

﴿فَإِنَّ مَعَ ٱلْعُسْرِ يُسْرًا ﴿٥﴾ إِنَّ مَعَ ٱلْعُسْرِ يُسْرًا ﴿٦﴾﴾ (سورة الشَّرح: ٥-٦)

﴾For surely with difficulty comes [a period of] ease. Surely with the difficulty comes [another period of] ease.﴿ *(Qur'an 94: 5-6)*

Despair

It is due to this reality that suicide is explicitly prohibited in Islam. Allah says in Chapter *an-Nisâ'*:

﴿... وَلَا تَقْتُلُوٓا۟ أَنفُسَكُمْ ۚ إِنَّ ٱللَّهَ كَانَ بِكُمْ رَحِيمًا ﴿٢٩﴾﴾ (سورة النِّسَاء: ٢٩)

﴿... Do not kill yourselves, indeed Allah is to you ever merciful.﴾ *(Qur'an 4: 29)*

Those who commit suicide are basically saying that God has burdened them beyond their capacity. They falsely accuse the Creator of treating them unfairly and thereby fall into a corrupt state of disbelief. Due to their rejection of faith, their thoughts about God become evil and they fall into utter despair. "Life," as they often say, "is so unfair that it is pointless to go on living."

﴿... إِنَّهُۥ لَا يَا۟يْـَٔسُ مِن رَّوْحِ ٱللَّهِ إِلَّا ٱلْقَوْمُ ٱلْكَـٰفِرُونَ ﴿٨٧﴾﴾

(سورة يُوسُف: ٨٧)

﴿... Indeed, no one despairs of relief from Allah except the disbelieving people.﴾ *(Qur'an 12: 87)*

Consequently, God has informed humankind that the punishment for those who harbor evil thoughts about Him is the eternal torment of hell. In Chapter *al-Fatḥ* Allah (ﷻ) says:

﴿وَيُعَذِّبَ ٱلْمُنَـٰفِقِينَ وَٱلْمُنَـٰفِقَـٰتِ وَٱلْمُشْرِكِينَ وَٱلْمُشْرِكَـٰتِ ٱلظَّآنِّينَ بِٱللَّهِ ظَنَّ ٱلسَّوْءِ ۚ عَلَيْهِمْ دَآئِرَةُ ٱلسَّوْءِ ۖ وَغَضِبَ ٱللَّهُ عَلَيْهِمْ وَلَعَنَهُمْ وَأَعَدَّ لَهُمْ جَهَنَّمَ ۖ وَسَآءَتْ مَصِيرًا ﴿٦﴾﴾ (سورة الفتح: ٦)

﴿That He may punish the hypocrites, men and women, and the polytheists, men and women, who harbor evil thoughts about

Allah. An evil torment will encompass them, for Allah is angry with them and curses them. And He has prepared hell for them; and evil it is as a destination.﴿ *(Qur'an 48: 6)*

Hope

On the other hand, the divine promises of justice and mercy fill the believers with the confidence necessary to patiently face the difficulties of this life. Consequently, hope in the mercy of God is an essential part of faith. Those who believe in Allah and patiently strive to do what is right have the right to hope for His mercy, for He has promised to help and support those who are patient:

﴾يَٰٓأَيُّهَا ٱلَّذِينَ ءَامَنُوا۟ ٱسْتَعِينُوا۟ بِٱلصَّبْرِ وَٱلصَّلَوٰةِ ۚ إِنَّ ٱللَّهَ مَعَ ٱلصَّٰبِرِينَ ﴿١٥٣﴾﴿

(سورة البقرة: ١٥٣)

﴾O' believers, seek help through patience and prayer. Truly, Allah is with the patient.﴿ *(Qur'an 2: 153)*

﴾إِنَّ ٱلَّذِينَ ءَامَنُوا۟ وَٱلَّذِينَ هَاجَرُوا۟ وَجَٰهَدُوا۟ فِى سَبِيلِ ٱللَّهِ أُو۟لَٰٓئِكَ يَرْجُونَ رَحْمَتَ ٱللَّهِ ۚ وَٱللَّهُ غَفُورٌ رَّحِيمٌ ﴿٢١٨﴾﴿

(سورة البقرة: ٢١٨)

﴾Surely those who believed, and those who emigrated and strove for the sake of Allah, hope for Allah's mercy, for Allah is Oft-Forgiving Most-Merciful.﴿ *(Qur'an 2: 218)*

Of course, Paradise is the reward for patience based on sincere belief in God. God informs the believers of their reward as follows:

﴾... وَبَشِّرِ ٱلصَّٰبِرِينَ ﴿١٥٥﴾ ٱلَّذِينَ إِذَآ أَصَٰبَتْهُم مُّصِيبَةٌ قَالُوٓا۟ إِنَّا لِلَّهِ وَإِنَّآ إِلَيْهِ رَٰجِعُونَ ﴿١٥٦﴾﴿

(سورة البقرة: ١٥٥-١٥٦)

﴿... So announce glad tidings [of Paradise] to the patient; those who, when afflicted with calamity, say: Truly we belong to Allah and to Him we will return.﴾ *(Qur'an 2: 155-6)*

Patience is also based on the belief that whatever befalls mankind is fundamentally a consequence of their own evil deeds.[8] God reminds humankind of this reality in Chapter *ash-Shoorâ* of the final revelation, saying:

﴿وَمَآ أَصَـٰبَكُم مِّن مُّصِيبَةٍ فَبِمَا كَسَبَتْ أَيْدِيكُمْ وَيَعْفُواْ عَن كَثِيرٍ ﴿٣٠﴾﴾

(سورة الشورى: ٣٠)

﴿Whatever befalls you of disaster is a result of what your hands have earned, but He pardons much.﴾ *(Qur'an 42: 30)*

The fact is, God has excused humans for much of their evil. Were He to punish them strictly according to their deeds, they and all on earth would be destroyed. God addresses this issue in Chapter *Fâṭir* as follows:

﴿وَلَوْ يُؤَاخِذُ ٱللَّهُ ٱلنَّاسَ بِمَا كَسَبُواْ مَا تَرَكَ عَلَىٰ ظَهْرِهَا مِن دَآبَّةٍ ... ﴿٤٥﴾﴾

(سورة فاطر: ٤٥)

﴿And if Allah were to punish people for what they earned, He would not leave a living creature on the face of the earth...﴾ *(Qur'an 35: 45)*

Consequently, both the trials of good and the tests of evil benefit the believer. The lives of the true believers are balanced between the extremes of human behavior. They neither become so happy with life's successes that they forget God, nor do they

---

[8] In fact, all of the corruption on earth is a product of human misdeeds. Allah states that in Chapter *ar-Room* (30):41, quoted later in this booklet.

become so depressed with life's difficulties and failures that they lose hope in God. Instead, they remember their Lord and Benefactor, and trust in His decisions. Ṣuhayb ibn Sinân related that the Messenger of Allah (ﷺ) said,

> "The affair of the believer is amazing! The whole of his life is beneficial, and that is only in the case of the believer. When good times come to him, he is thankful and it is good for him, and when bad times befall him, he is patient and it is also good for him."[9]

This is the state of one who has accepted God's destiny. Consequently, belief in both the good and the apparent evil of what has been destined is the sixth pillar of faith in Islam.

On the other hand, if the believers experience a life devoid of any problems, it should be taken as a sign that something is wrong. Under such circumstances, the true believer must take time out and reflect on the realities of his or her life. Either the tests are not obvious and they are unaware of them or they have deviated from the right path. Allah (ﷻ) informs the believers in Chapter *at-Tawbah* that the apparent enjoyment which the disbelievers take from their great wealth and children is only a prelude to their punishment.

﴿وَلَا تُعْجِبْكَ أَمْوَٰلُهُمْ وَأَوْلَٰدُهُمْ ۚ إِنَّمَا يُرِيدُ ٱللَّهُ أَن يُعَذِّبَهُم بِهَا فِى ٱلدُّنْيَا وَتَزْهَقَ أَنفُسُهُمْ وَهُمْ كَٰفِرُونَ ﴿٨٥﴾﴾ (سورة التوبة: ٨٥)

﴿Do not be impressed by their wealth or their children. Allah only wishes to punish them with these things in this life and that their souls should depart while they are disbelievers.﴾ *(Qur'an 9: 85)*

---

[9] *Ṣaḥeeḥ Muslim*, vol. 4, p. 1541, hadith no. 7138.

This is not to say that the believers should yearn for problems and calamities in their lives, for Allah has taught them to pray: ﴾Our Lord, do not put on us a burden like what You placed on those before us.﴿[10] Instead, they should thank Allah for whatever trials He has spared them. However, in times of ease they must remain vigilant and not become oblivious to tests, for success and happiness often blind people to the trials of life.

Reminder

Tests sometimes serve as a punishing reminder to those who have gone astray and an encouragement for them to return to the correct path. When people deviate, they seldom listen to the advice of those around them. However, when a calamity strikes them or those near and dear to them, it jolts those who still have some faith into recognizing their error.

﴿وَلَنُذِيقَنَّهُم مِّنَ ٱلْعَذَابِ ٱلْأَدْنَىٰ دُونَ ٱلْعَذَابِ ٱلْأَكْبَرِ لَعَلَّهُمْ يَرْجِعُونَ ﴿٢١﴾﴾ (سورة السجدة: ٢١)

﴾And We[11] will surely let them taste the nearer punishment short of the greater punishment that perhaps they will return [i.e., repent].﴿ *(Qur'an 32: 21)*

The test of calamities which remind humankind of their deviation may come in the form of man's inhumanity to his fellow man, as in the case of the unspeakable atrocities unleashed by the Serbs against the Bosnian Muslims who had strayed far away from Islam, or Saddam's brutal invasion of Kuwait and America's

---

[10] *Soorat al-Baqarah* (2):286.

[11] "We" in the original Arabic is the majestic 'we,' referring to God.

subsequent indiscriminate bombing of civilian targets in Iraq. Allah points out that whatever humans suffer at the hands of other humans, they brought it upon themselves. However, the suffering is a reminder to return to the path of righteousness.

﴿ظَهَرَ ٱلْفَسَادُ فِي ٱلْبَرِّ وَٱلْبَحْرِ بِمَا كَسَبَتْ أَيْدِي ٱلنَّاسِ لِيُذِيقَهُم بَعْضَ ٱلَّذِي عَمِلُوا۟ لَعَلَّهُمْ يَرْجِعُونَ ﴿٤١﴾﴾ (سورة الرُّوم: ٤١)

﴿Corruption has appeared on the land and in the sea because of what man's hands have earned, in order that [Allah] may make them taste a part of what they have done, and in order that they may return [to the right path].﴾ *(Qur'an 30: 41)*

Hypocrisy

Calamities also expose those who falsely claim faith, as well as show those who disbelieve that they choose hell by their own free will. There have been many cases of people converting to Islam for the wrong reasons, and after finding more difficulties in their lives than prior to their conversion, they revert to their former beliefs. God states in Chapter *al-'Ankaboot* of the final revelation:

﴿أَحَسِبَ ٱلنَّاسُ أَن يُتْرَكُوٓا۟ أَن يَقُولُوٓا۟ ءَامَنَّا وَهُمْ لَا يُفْتَنُونَ ﴿٢﴾ وَلَقَدْ فَتَنَّا ٱلَّذِينَ مِن قَبْلِهِمْ ۖ فَلَيَعْلَمَنَّ ٱللَّهُ ٱلَّذِينَ صَدَقُوا۟ وَلَيَعْلَمَنَّ ٱلْكَٰذِبِينَ ﴿٣﴾﴾

(سورة العَنكبوت: ٢-٣)

﴿Do people imagine that they will be left to say, "We believe" and they will not be tried? But We[12] have certainly tried those before

[12] "We" in the original Arabic is the majestic 'we,' referring to God.

them, and Allah willl surely make evident those who are truthful, and He will surely make evident the liars.﴿ *(Qur'an 29: 2-3)*

Punishment

Those who transgress the limits set by God expose themselves to punishment in this life and the next. Throughout the Qur'an, Allah describes numerous past nations who rejected divine guidance and were subsequently destroyed. These stories serve as warnings to humanity of the consequences of rebellion against the commandments of God. In Chapter *an-Noor*, Allah gives a general warning as follows:

﴿... فَلْيَحْذَرِ ٱلَّذِينَ يُخَالِفُونَ عَنْ أَمْرِهِۦٓ أَن تُصِيبَهُمْ فِتْنَةٌ أَوْ يُصِيبَهُمْ عَذَابٌ أَلِيمٌ ﴿٦٣﴾﴾

(سورة النّور: ٦٣)

﴾... So let those who dissent from his command beware of a trial or a painful punishment.﴿ *(Qur'an 24: 63)*

The punishment may come in a variety of different ways. Perhaps the most obvious punishment afflicting humankind in all countries today is the disease AIDS,[13] which appeared for the first time in medical history in the beginning of the '80's.[14] The vast majority of those who are affected by it around the globe are the promiscuous. Initially homosexuals were the main victims, then bisexuals, followed by promiscuous heterosexuals and

---

[13] Acquired immune deficiency syndrome (AIDS) is a condition transmitted by a virus which attacks the body's system of defence against disease, leaving the sufferer extremely vulnerable to disease and likely to die eventually from any one that he or she catches. (*Chambers Pocket Dictionary*, p. 19.)

[14] It was first identified in 1981. (*The New Encyclopaedia Britannica*, vol. 10, p. 676.)

intravenous drug users. All of these groups were in open rebellion against the divine laws that restrict sexual relations to males and females within the bounds of marriage and those laws that prohibit the use of intoxicants. Some may point out that AIDS was also spread to chaste individuals through blood transfusions and to children by their parents. However, medical statistics show that such cases are relatively few in comparison to the other categories. In any case, Allah has warned in Chapter *al-Anfâl* of the final revelation that when His punishment comes it is not limited to the sinful, but it may affect the entire society.

﴿وَٱتَّقُوا۟ فِتْنَةً لَّا تُصِيبَنَّ ٱلَّذِينَ ظَلَمُوا۟ مِنكُمْ خَآصَّةً ۖ وَٱعْلَمُوٓا۟ أَنَّ ٱللَّهَ شَدِيدُ ٱلْعِقَابِ ﴿٢٥﴾﴾ (سورة الأنفال: ٢٥)

﴿Beware of a trial which will not afflict only the sinful among you, and know that Allah is severe in punishment.﴾ *(Qur'an 8: 25)*

One thousand four hundred years ago, Prophet Muhammad (ﷺ) prophesied the coming of such a trial. Ibn 'Umar quoted him as saying,

> "Whenever promiscuity is openly practiced among a people, a plague and anguish will spread among them which was unknown to their predecessors."[15]

However, AIDS is only one in a series of diseases. Before AIDS, a warning came in the form of another disease called herpes, which became widespread among the sexually promiscuous beginning in the 1960s and '70s. It was declared an epidemic in America in the mid-seventies, and there is no known cure for it until today.

---

[15] Collected by Ibn Mâjah and authenticated in *Ṣaḥeeḥ Sunan Ibn Mâjah*, vol. 2, p. 370, hadith no. 3246.

People's attention switched from it by the end of the '70s because it was not fatal,[16] while AIDS was.

---

[16] When symptoms occur, fever and malaise are followed by burning pain in the genital area and enlargement of the lymph nodes in the groin. Blisters and small ulcers are usually found in the area of infection, and there is severe pain and burning upon urination. (*The New Encyclopaedia Britannica*, vol. 21, p. 536.)

WHY DID GOD CREATE THE WORLD?

The purpose, relative to humankind, for which the world and its contents were created is specifically defined in the final revelation. Allah says in Chapters *Ibrâheem* and *al-An'âm*:

﴿ٱللَّهُ ٱلَّذِى خَلَقَ ٱلسَّمَٰوَٰتِ وَٱلْأَرْضَ وَأَنزَلَ مِنَ ٱلسَّمَآءِ مَآءً فَأَخْرَجَ بِهِۦ مِنَ ٱلثَّمَرَٰتِ رِزْقًا لَّكُمْ ۖ وَسَخَّرَ لَكُمُ ٱلْفُلْكَ لِتَجْرِىَ فِى ٱلْبَحْرِ بِأَمْرِهِۦ ۖ وَسَخَّرَ لَكُمُ ٱلْأَنْهَٰرَ ﴿٣٢﴾ وَسَخَّرَ لَكُمُ ٱلشَّمْسَ وَٱلْقَمَرَ دَآئِبَيْنِ ۖ وَسَخَّرَ لَكُمُ ٱلَّيْلَ وَٱلنَّهَارَ ﴿٣٣﴾﴾ (سورة إبراهيم: ٣٢-٣٣)

﴿Allah is the One Who created the heavens and the earth and sent down rain from the sky and with it brought out fruit for your provision. He has put ships in your service, sailing through the sea by His command; and likewise He has put the rivers in your service. He has also put the sun and moon in their orbits to be of service to you; and He made the night and day in your service.﴾

(Qur'an, 14: 32-33)

﴿فَالِقُ ٱلْإِصْبَاحِ وَجَعَلَ ٱلَّيْلَ سَكَنًا وَٱلشَّمْسَ وَٱلْقَمَرَ حُسْبَانًا ۚ ذَٰلِكَ تَقْدِيرُ ٱلْعَزِيزِ ٱلْعَلِيمِ ﴿٩٦﴾ وَهُوَ ٱلَّذِى جَعَلَ لَكُمُ ٱلنُّجُومَ لِتَهْتَدُوا۟ بِهَا فِى ظُلُمَٰتِ ٱلْبَرِّ وَٱلْبَحْرِ ۗ قَدْ فَصَّلْنَا ٱلْءَايَٰتِ لِقَوْمٍ يَعْلَمُونَ ﴿٩٧﴾﴾ (سورة الأنعام: ٩٦-٩٧)

﴿He is the Cleaver of the daybreak and has made the night for rest and the sun and moon for calculation. That is the determination of the Exalted in Might, the Knowing. And it is He Who placed for you the stars that you may be guided by them through the darknesses of the land and sea. We have detailed the signs for a people who know.﴿ *(Qur'an 6: 96-7)*

The contents of this world were created for the service of humankind. Whether they are products of man's invention, like ships, or they are nature itself, all have been granted by God for the benefit of human beings. However, such gifts are not without responsibility. Humans are required to recognize Allah's bounties and mercies and give thanks to Him and glorify him. For example, He taught the believers in Chapter *az-Zukhruf* to pray as follows whenever they ride an animal or vehicle: ﴾That you may settle yourselves upon their backs and then remember the favour of your Lord when you have settled upon them and say, 'Exalted is He Who has subjected this to us, and we could not have [otherwise] subdued it. And indeed we, to our Lord, will [surely] return.'﴿ *(Qur'an 43: 13-14)*

Human beings also carry the responsibility to govern the creation according to the laws of God. This is man's purpose relative to the rest of creation. They are commanded to utilize the contents of this world according to the laws of God. Abu Sa'eed al-Khudri quoted Allah's Messenger (ﷺ) as saying,

> "The world is beautiful and green, and Allah — be He exalted — has made you governors over it to see how you will act."[1]

Human beings are not free to do with the world as they please. Consequently, the negative attitude of secular materialist society towards nature is contrary to divine revelation.

---

[1] *Ṣaḥeeḥ Muslim*, vol. 4, p. 1432, hadith no. 6606.

Materialist society regards nature as an enemy to be conquered. It is not enough to appreciate the beauty of mount Everest, instead, lives have to be lost every year in 'conquering' it by climbing to its summit. It is not sufficient to marvel at the exotic animals of the world, instead, during the safaris of the past century, many of these animals were hunted into extinction to provide trophies for Western living rooms. Although safaris have now been stopped, the reduced numbers of animals like the rhinoceros continue to be threatened with extinction due to the importance of their horns as an ingredient for Far Eastern traditional medicines and aphrodisiacs.

Animals

According to the final revelation, killing animals for sport is forbidden and sinful in the sight of God. Ibn 'Abbâs reported the Messenger of Allah (ﷺ) as saying,

"Do not take as a target any living thing."[2]

Taking the life of any living animal is prohibited unless it is for food, for protection of human life, or for clothing. Killing for fun and enjoyment is fundamentally evil. And, even when the life of a human is taken for crimes against society, or the life of an animal is taken for food, it must be done as painlessly as possible. Shaddâd ibn Aws recounted two things which he remembered the Messenger of Allah (ﷺ) saying,

---

[2] *Ṣaḥeeḥ Muslim*, vol. 3, p. 1079, hadith no. 4813. Hishâm ibn Zayd reported that when he and his grandfather, Anas ibn Mâlik, visited the home of Ḥakam ibn Ayyoob, (they saw) some people using a hen as a target for their arrows. Anas related that Allah's Messenger had forbidden the tying of animals (as targets). *Ṣaḥeeḥ Muslim*, vol. 3, p. 1078, hadith no. 4182.

> "Surely Allah has enjoined goodness for everything; so when you execute someone, do so in a good way and when you slaughter an animal, do so in a good way. Let every one of you sharpen his knife and allow the slaughtered animal to die comfortably."[3]

Although some 'animal lovers' in Western countries have opposed the Islamic method of slaughtering animals, the Western alternative of stunning the animals by electric shock or crushing blows to the head are far more painful to the animals. When the neck is cut by an extremely sharp knife, the animal does not feel it and quickly loses consciousness as the heart pumps its blood out of the carotid arteries.

Caring for animals is enshrined in the divine law, even in the case of dogs, which are generally barred from Muslim homes.[4] Abu Hurayrah (رضي الله عنه) quoted the Prophet (ﷺ) as saying,

> "A man became thirsty while walking, so he climbed down a well and drank from it. On coming out he saw a thirsty dog panting and eating mud. The man said (to himself), 'This animal is as thirsty as I was.' So he climbed down the well and filled his shoe with water. He then held his shoe between his teeth, climbed out and gave the dog water. Allah thanked him and forgave him (and put him in Paradise)."[5] The people asked, "O' Messenger of Allah!

---

[3] *Ṣaḥeeḥ Muslim*, vol. 3, p. 1078, no. 4810.

[4] Muslims are discouraged from keeping dogs as pets. However, guard dogs, sheep dogs and hunting dogs are permitted. Ibn 'Umar quoted Allah's Messenger (ﷺ) as saying, "Whoever keeps a dog for other than watching the herd or hunting, will lose the weight of two mountains from his [scale of good] deeds daily." (*Ṣaḥeeḥ Muslim*, vol. 3, p. 826, hadith no. 3815.)

[5] *Ṣaḥeeḥ al-Bukhari,* vol. 1, p. 120, hadith no. 174.

> Do we get a reward for serving animals?" He replied, "In (the service of) every living being there is a reward."[6]

Abu Hurayrah also narrated that Allah's Messenger (ﷺ) said,

> "Allah forgave a prostitute (among the Israelites)[7] who tied her shoe to her scarf and drew out some water (from a well) for a dog that she saw dying of thirst. Because of that, Allah forgave her."[8]

Conversely, harming animals is a major sin according to Islamic law. 'Abdullâh ibn 'Umar related that the Messenger of Allah (ﷺ) said,

> "A woman was punished and placed in Hell because of a cat which she imprisoned until it died. She neither gave it food nor water, nor did she set it free to eat from the rodents of the earth."[9]

There are circumstances where it is necessary to inflict pain on animals, such as hitting animals to get them to move and branding them for identification. However, even in these situations, God gave instructions to protect them. Jâbir (رضي الله عنه) reported that,

> "The Prophet (ﷺ) prohibited striking animals in their faces or branding them on their faces."[10]

---

[6] *Ṣaḥeeḥ al-Bukhari*, vol. 3, pp. 322-3, hadith no. 551, and *Ṣaḥeeḥ Muslim*, vol. 4, Pp. 1215-6, hadith no. 5577.

[7] *Ṣaḥeeḥ al-Bukhari*, vol. 4, Pp. 448-9, hadith no. 673.

[8] *Ṣaḥeeḥ al-Bukhari*, vol. 4, Pp. 338-9, hadith no. 538, and *Ṣaḥeeḥ Muslim*, vol. 4, p. 1216, hadith no. 5579.

[9] *Ṣaḥeeḥ al-Bukhari*, vol. 4, p. 456, hadith no. 689, and *Ṣaḥeeḥ Muslim*, vol. 4, p. 1215, hadith no. 5573.

[10] *Ṣaḥeeḥ Muslim*, vol. 3, p. 1163, hadith no. 5281.

Vegetation

Humankind's responsibility of looking after this world does not stop at serving animals. The vegetable kingdom is also highly regarded in divine law. So much so, that Muslims engaged in war are forbidden to destroy fruit trees,[11] and even the planting of trees is considered an act of charity. Jâbir quoted Allah's Messenger (ﷺ) as saying,

> "Any Muslim who plants a tree gains the reward of giving in charity. What is eaten from it is charity, what is stolen from it, what the animals eat and what the birds eat, is all charity. Anyone or anything that takes from it earns for the planter the reward of [giving in] charity."[12]

Islam encourages that no effort should be spared in planting, even if it becomes the last thing that the believer can do in this life. Anas (رضي الله عنه) related that the Prophet (ﷺ) said,

> "If the (signs of) the beginning of the Day of Resurrection appear and one of you has a seedling in his hand, he should plant it if he is able to do so before the resurrection begins."[13]

Consequently, human beings have a responsibility to look after all aspects of the environment in which they were created as a sacred duty to God. This requires an active opposition to the massive pollution and destruction of natural habitats caused by today's

---

[11] *Muwaṭṭa' Imam Mâlik*, p. 200, hadith no. 958, and authenticated by Shaykh al-Albâni in *I'rwâ' al-Ghaleel*, vol. 5, p. 13-4, hadith no. 1190.

[12] *Ṣaḥeeḥ Muslim*, vol. 3, p. 818, hadith no. 3764.

[13] Collected by Aḥmad in *al-Musnad*, vol. 3, Pp. 183, 184 and 191, and Bukhari in *al-Adab al-Mufrad*, no. 479, and authenticated by Shaykh al-Albâni in *Silsilat al-Aḥâdeeth aṣ-Ṣaḥeeḥah*, vol. 1, p. 11, hadith no. 9.

materialistic, consumer societies the world over. According to revelation, negligence of this duty is considered a sin while fulfillment of it is an act of worship.

CONCLUSION

Without knowledge of the purpose of creation, human beings wander aimlessly through life, like ships at sea without rudders. Their goals are either wrong due to incorrect religious teachings, or materialistic and thus confined to this world. It is, therefore, essential for their own well-being that they know why God created them.

Fundamentally, Allah created in order to manifest His attributes. Consequently, creation is the consequence of His being the Creator, paradise manifests His Mercy and Grace, hell His Justice, humankind's errors His Forgiveness, living and non-living beings His Generosity, etc. The significance of knowing that creation is a means by which Allah manifests His attributes is that human beings can then correctly recognize God and accept His decree and their destiny. However, it is of even greater importance that human beings know the purpose for which they were created. The final Revelation teaches that it is to worship God because humankind must worship Him in order to attain righteousness and the spiritual status necessary to enter paradise. The significance of this knowledge is that human beings understand that worship is as much a necessity as eating and breathing and that it is not a favor they are doing for God.

It is also essential that human beings grasp the importance of this world's bounties and trials. Without knowledge of the purpose behind their creation, humans tend to look at this world as being hostile to them. However, God created it primarily for their benefit. The tests of good and evil are designed to bring out the higher spiritual qualities of the human being. However, humans are not able to benefit from the tests unless they put complete trust in God and have patience in what He has destined for them. For those who reject God, the trials of this world become a punishment for them in this life prior to the eternal punishment in the next world.

Knowledge of the purpose of the world also makes the believer environmentally conscious. Humankind is responsible to utilize the bounties of this life justly. The creatures of the earth and seas, the vegetation and the atmosphere have been put in his care. Consequently, humans should take great care to preserve the environment and the living creatures within it as a means of giving thanks to God.

With such a comprehensive consciousness of purpose, human beings become whole. They are transformed into guides for humankind, showing the way to righteousness. Consequently, Allah describes them as the best of mankind in the final revelation:

﴿كُنتُمْ خَيْرَ أُمَّةٍ أُخْرِجَتْ لِلنَّاسِ تَأْمُرُونَ بِالْمَعْرُوفِ وَتَنْهَوْنَ عَنِ الْمُنكَرِ وَتُؤْمِنُونَ بِاللَّهِ ... ﴿١١٠﴾﴾ (سورة آل عِمرَان: ١١٠)

﴿You are the best nation produced for mankind because you command righteousness, forbid evil and believe in Allah...﴾

(Qur'an 3: 110)

INDEX OF HADITH

INDEX OF QUR'ANIC VERSES

"I have not created the jinn and humankind except to worship Me..." *(51: 56)* 32

"Indeed, I am Allah, there is no deity except Me, so worship Me..." *(20: 14)* 36

"Indeed, it is by the remembrance of Allah..." *(13: 28)* 57

"Indeed, no one despairs of relief from Allah..." *(12: 87)* 60

"Indeed, the creation of the heavens and the earth is greater..." *(40: 57)* 19

"Indeed, the religion in the sight of Allah is Islam." *(3: 19)* 39

"[It is He] who created death and life to test which..." *(67: 2)* 51

"Indeed, those you [polytheists] call upon besides Allah..." *(7: 194)* 48

"Know that your property and children are but a trial." *(8: 28)* 53

"No calamity strikes except by Allah's permission." *(64: 11)* 22

"O' believers! Do not allow your wealth and children..." *(63: 9)* 53

"O' believers! Remember Allah often." *(33: 41)* 36

"O' believers, seek help through patience and prayer." *(2: 153)* 61

"O' you who believed, decreed upon you is fasting..." *(2: 183)* 36

SYMBOLS DIRECTORY

(سبحانه وتعالى) : *Subḥânahu wa Ta'âla* — "The Exalted."

(صلى الله عليه وسلم) : *Ṣalla-Allâhu 'Alayhi wa Sallam* — "Blessings and peace be upon him."

(عليه السلام) : *'Alayhis-Salâm* — "May peace be upon him."

(رضي الله عنه) : *Raḍia-Allâhu 'Anhu* — "May Allah be pleased with him."

(رضي الله عنها) : *Raḍia-Allâhu 'Anha* — "May Allah be pleased with her."

BIBLIOGRAPHY

Albâni, Nâṣirud-Deen al-, *I'rwâ' al-Ghaleel*, Beirut: Al-Maktab al-Islami, 1st ed., 1979.

——————, *Ṣaḥeeḥ Sunan Abu Dawood,* Beirut: Al-Maktab al-Islami, 1st ed., 1988.

——————, *Ṣaḥeeḥ Sunan at-Tirmidhi*, Riyadh: Arab Bureau of Education for the Gulf States, 1st ed., 1988.

——————, *Ṣaḥeeḥ Sunan ibn Mâjah*, Beirut: Al-Maktab al-Islami, 3rd ed., 1988.

——————, *Silsilat al-Aḥâdeeth aṣ-Ṣaḥeeḥah,* vol. 1, Beirut: Al-Maktab al-Islami, 4th ed., 1985.

——————, *Silsilat al-Aḥâdeeth aṣ-Ṣaḥeeḥah,* vol. 4, Riyadh: Maktabat al-Ma'ârif, 4th ed., 1988.

Chambers Pocket Dictionary, Edinburgh: W&R Chambers, 1992.

Ḥasan, Aḥmad, *Sunan Abu Dawood* (English), Lahore: Sh. Muhammad Ashraf Publishers, 1st ed., 1984.

Khan, Muhammad Muḥsin, *Ṣaḥeeḥ al-Bukhari*, (Arabic-English), Riyadh: Maktabat ar-Riyâḍ al-Ḥadeethah, 1981.

Rahimuddin, Muhammad, *Muwaṭṭa' Imam Mâlik* (English), Lahore: Sh. Muhammad Ashraf, 1980.

Reese, W.L., Dictionary of Philosophy and Religion, New Jersey: Humanities Press, 1980.

Robson, James, *Mishkat al-Maṣâbeeḥ*, Lahore: Sh. Muhammad Ashraf, 1981.

Ṣiddiq, ‘Abdul Hamid, *Ṣaḥeeḥ Muslim* (English), Lahore: Sh. Muhammad Ashraf Publishers, 1987.

The Living Webster Encyclopaedic Dictionary, Chicago: The English Language Institute of America, 1975.

The New Encyclopaedia Britannica, Chicago: Encyclopaedia Britannica, 15th ed., 1991.

The World Book Encyclopaedia, Chicago: World Book, 1987.

GLOSSARY

Âl 'Imrân	آل عمران :	Lit.: The family of 'Imrân; name of the 3rd *soorah* of the Qur'an
'Abd	عَبْد :	Slave, servant
Adh-Dhâriyat	الذّاريات :	Lit.: The scattering winds; name of the 51st *soorah* of the Qur'an
Al-Aḥzâb	الأحزاب :	Lit.: The parties. The combined forces-referring to the alliance of disbelieving Arab tribes against the Muslims; name of the 33rd *soorah* of the Qur'an
Al-Anfâl	الأنفال :	The bounties, spoils of war; name of the 8th *soorah* of the Qur'an
Aḥâdeeth	أحاديث :	Sing.: Hadith; Records of Prophetic sayings and doings etc.
Al-Anbiyâ'	الأنبياء :	Sing.: *an-Nabi*; The Prophets
Al-An'âm	الأنعام :	The Grazing Livestock, i.e., camels, cattle, etc.; name of the 6th *soorah* of the Qur'an
Al-'Ankaboot	العنكبوت :	The Spider; name of the 29th *soorah* of the Qur'an
Al-Baqarah	البقرة :	The Cow; name of the 2nd *soorah* of the Qur'an

Al-Bayinah	البيِّنة	Clear Evidence; name of the 98th *soorah* of the Qur'an
Al-Falaq	الفَلَق	Daybreak; name of the 113rd *soorah* of the Qur'an
Al-Fatḥ	الفتح	The Conquest; name of the 48th *soorah* of the Qur'an
Al-Furqân	الفُرقان	The Criterion (another name for the Qur'an which distinguishes truth from falsehood); name of the 25th *soorah* of the Qur'an
Al-Inshirâḥ or (ash-Sharḥ)	الانشراح أو الشّرح	Expansion; name of the 94th *soorah* of the Qur'an
Al-Isrâ'	الإسراء	The Night Journey; name of the 17th *soorah* of the Qur'an
Al-Kahf	الكهف	The Cave; name of the 18th *soorah* of the Qur'an
Al-Mâ'idah	المائدة	The Table (referring to the table spread with food requested by the disciples of Jesus (may peace be upon him); name of the 5th *soorah* of the Qur'an
Al-Mujâdilah	المُجادلة	The Arguing (or Pleading) Woman; name of the 58th *soorah* of the Qur'an
Al-Mulk	المُلْك	Dominion; name of the 67th *soorah* of the Qur'an
Al-Munâfiqoon	المُنافِقون	The Hypocrites; name of the 63rd *soorah* of the Qur'an

An-Naḥl	النَّحل :	The Bees (Sing.: *Naḥlah*: Bee); name of the 16th *soorah* of the Qur'an
An-Naml	النَّمل :	The Ants (Sing.: *Namlah*: Ant); name of the 27th *soorah* of the Qur'an
An-Naṣr	النَّصْر :	The Victory; name of the 110th *soorah* of the Qur'an
An-Nisâ'	النِّساء :	The Women (Sing.: *Imra'ah*: Woman); name of the 4th *soorah* of the Qur'an
An-Noor	النّور :	Light; name of the 24th *soorah* of the Qur'an
Ar-Ra'd	الرَّعْد :	Thunder; name of the 13th *soorah* of the Qur'an
Ar-Room	الرُّوم :	The Byzantines (or Romaeans); name of the 30th *soorah* of the Qur'an
Ash-Shoorâ	الشُورى :	Consultation, Counselling; name of the 42nd *soorah* of the Qur'an
As-Sajdah	السّجدة :	Prostration; name of the 32nd *soorah* of the Qur'an
Az-Zukhruf	الزّخرف :	Ornament; name of the 43rd *soorah* of the Qur'an
Bismillâh	بسم اللّه :	In the Name of Allah (The Glorified, The Exalted)
Fâṭir	فاطر :	The Creator, Originator (of Creation); name of the 35th *soorah* of the Qur'an

Fitnah	فِتنة :	Trial, affliction, temptation
Ghâfir	غافِر :	Forgiver, i.e., Allah (The Glorious, The Exalted); name of the 40th *soorah* of the Qur'an
'Ibâdah	عِبادة :	Worship
Ibrâheem	إبراهيم :	Prophet Abraham (may peace be upon him); name of the 14th *soorah* of the Qur'an
Kâfir	كافِر :	Unbeliever, disbeliever
Mishkât	مِشكاة :	Niche
Maṣâbeeḥ	مصابيح :	Lamps (Sing.: *Miṣbâḥ*: Lamp)
Shirk	شِرْك :	Polytheism, associating partners with Allah
Soorah	سورة :	Chapter of the Qur'an
Sunan	سُنَن :	Sing.: Sunnah; Lit.: Ways/ traditions; It refers to the ways of the Prophet Muhammad, Blessings and peace be upon him
Zakâh	زكاة :	Poor due or obligatory charity tax. Muslim whose wealth is above a certain limit must pay a percentage of it (in most cases 2.5%) to the poor and needy. Zakah is one of the pillar of Islam